For sale by the Superintendent of Documents, U.S. Government Printing Office
Washington, DC 20402

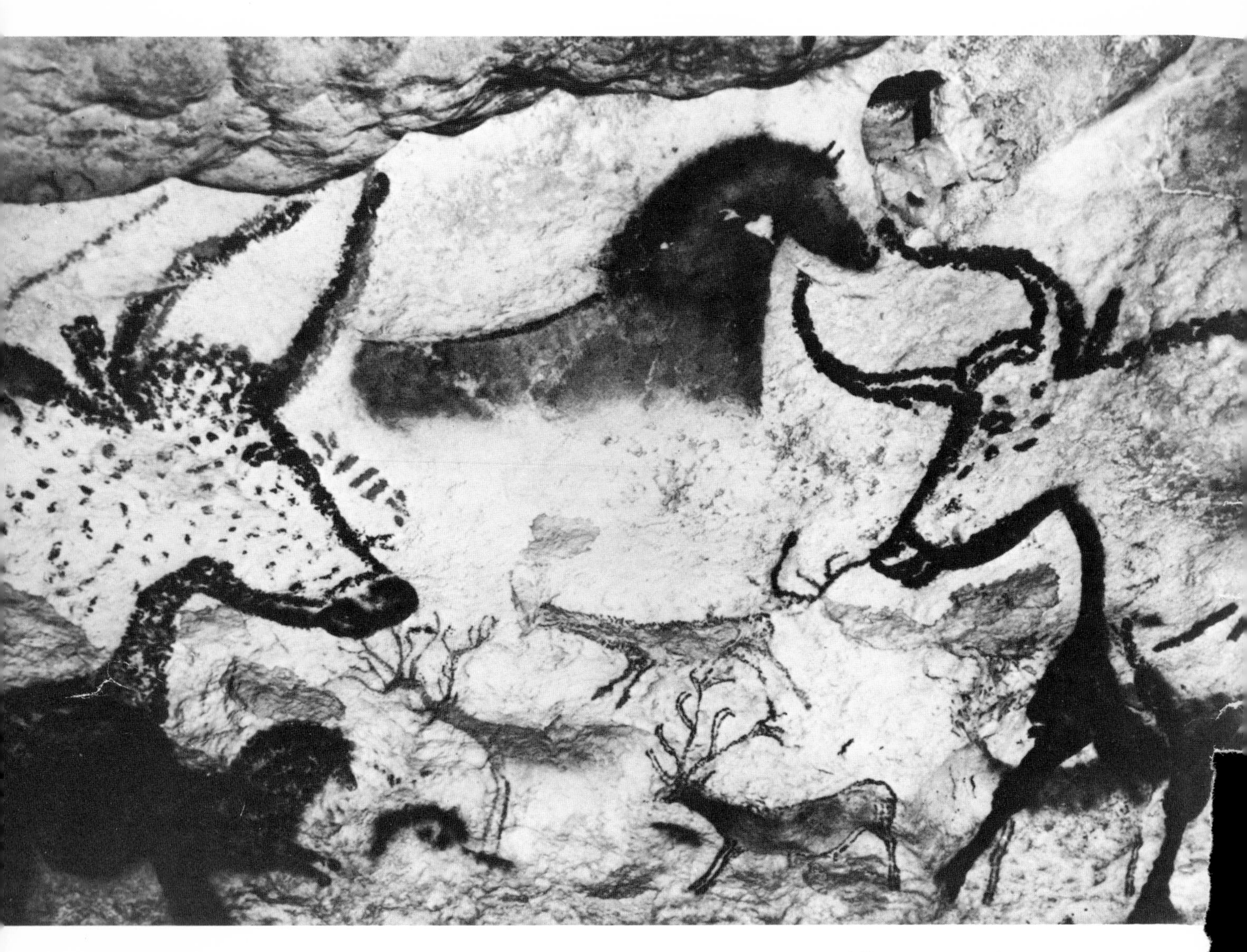

Painting from the Lascaux Caves, courtesy of the French Government Tourist Office, New York

Toward Civilization

A Report on Arts Education

National Endowment for the Arts

May 1988

PHOTO CREDITS

On the Cover: (Left to right, beginning on back cover, each column from bottom to top)

1. Montgomery County (Maryland) Public Schools, William Mills, photographer.

2. *Painting from the Lascaux Caves* (Detail), courtesy of the French Government Tourist Office, New York. *Bust of Queen Nofretete* (Detail), Egyptisches Museum, SMPK, Berlin (West).

3. *Parthenon,* Athens, courtesy of the Greek National Tourist Organization. *Amiens Cathedral,* courtesy of the French Government Tourist Office, New York.

4. *Aztec Calendar Stone* (Stone of the Sun), Museo Nacional, Mexico City, National Archives #66-G-10A-24, Washington. William Shakespeare, *Title Page of First Folio,* The Folger Shakespeare Library, Washington.

5. *Head of an Oba,* National Museum of African Art, Smithsonian Institution, Eliot Elisofon Archives, Washington. Rembrandt van Rijn, *Self-Portrait* (Detail), National Gallery of Art, Andrew W. Mellon Collection, Washington.

6. Gilbert Stuart, *George Washington* (Detail), National Portrait Gallery, Smithsonian Institution, Washington, owned jointly with the Museum of Fine Arts, Boston. Franz Schubert, *Impromptus, Piano* D.899, (Detail), page 1, The Pierpont Morgan Library, New York. *A Girl at the End of a Small Boat Landing with a Maidservant Who Lights the Way* (Detail), Japanese, Edo Period, Ukiyoe School, courtesy of the The Freer Gallery of Art, Smithsonian Institution, Washington.

7. Samuel Clemens (Mark Twain), *Adventures of Huckleberry Finn.* Title Page, 1885, First American edition, H.883, The Pierpont Morgan Library, New York. *Basket,* Shoshonean, Fernandinos Mission, California, before 1920, Smithsonian Institution, Department of Anthropology, cat. #64687, Washington.

8. Charlie Chaplin in *The Kid,* courtesy of The American Film Institute, Washington. Drawing of a television set, by Michael Sawyer, Washington. Martha Graham, photograph by Barbara Morgan, courtesy of the Martha Graham Dance Company, New York.

9. Pablo Picasso, *Guernica* (Detail), Museo del Prado, Madrid. Marian Anderson in the 1930's, National Archives photo #208-PU-5A-2, Washington. Benny Goodman, photograph by Michael Wilderman, courtesy of Festival Productions, Inc. Frank Lloyd Wright, *Fallingwater,* photo courtesy of Western Pennsylvania Conservancy, Harold Corsini, photographer. Still photograph from the movie *A Streetcar Named Desire,* permission from copyright owner secured by Edelman Enterprises. Montgomery County (Maryland) Public Schools, William Mills, photographer.

The National Endowment for the Arts, an independent agency of the Federal government, was created in 1965 to encourage and support American arts and artists. Its mission — to foster the excellence, diversity, and vitality of the arts and to help broaden the availability and appreciation of such excellence — is carried out by awarding grants and by providing leadership and advocacy in the field of the arts. Questions or comments regarding this publication may be directed to the National Endowment for the Arts, Arts in Education Program, 1100 Pennsylvania Avenue, N.W., Washington, D.C. 20506.

Library of Congress Cataloging-in-Publication Data

National Endowment for the Arts.
Toward civilization: a report on arts education/National Endowment for the Arts.
p. cm.
"May 1988."
Bibliography: p.
1. Arts — Study and teaching — United States. I. Title.
NX303.N38 1988 88-15499
707'.073 — dc19 CIP

- Those who believe the arts should be a basic part of education should work together to develop consensus on the purpose and content of arts education. They must make the case for arts education being a fundamental *educational* responsibility. Ensuring comprehensive and sequential arts education calls for greater political effort than would be necessary for subjects currently assumed to be basic.

- The National Endowment for the Arts should continue and strengthen its arts education efforts over at least the next 10-year period. Endowment efforts to date have set the agency on this course. It will take time, however, to make the case for arts education, facilitate state and local collaborations, and help develop and distribute curricular, instructional, and assessment models. The Endowment should continue its efforts to develop a television series on the arts for young people.

This report builds on thousands of hours of research and consultation and benefits from the advice of many of those dedicated to the cause of arts education. We are indebted to Congress for requesting the report and in particular for the leadership of Representatives Pat Williams, E. Thomas Coleman, Sidney R. Yates and Ralph Regula, and Senators Claiborne Pell, Robert T. Stafford, Robert C. Byrd, and James A. McClure. We are also grateful for the wise counsel of the members of the National Council on the Arts and the Endowment's Advisory Committee on Arts Education. We wish to thank the U.S. Department of Education, Secretary William J. Bennett and his counselor Chester E. Finn, Jr., without whose cooperation this report would not have been possible. We also thank Professor Brent Wilson of Pennsylvania State University who gave up a summer in Europe to help us with the report.

Finally, I would like to thank many of the Endowment staff for their hard work and assistance. Whatever deficiencies there may be in the report are mine.

Frank Hodsoll
Chairman
National Endowment for the Arts

Contents

Aztec Calendar Stone (Stone of the Sun), Museo Nacional, Mexico City, National Archives #66-G-10A-24, Washington

Preface

THE CONGRESSIONAL MANDATE

In 1985, the 99th Congress called for a "study of the state of arts education" as part of the reauthorization of the National Endowment for the Arts. This was the second such request in history. The first, more than a hundred years ago, was a request by the 46th Congress for the report, *Art and Industry, Instruction in Drawing Applied to Industrial and Fine Arts,* which was completed by Isaac Edwards Clarke in 1884. That report reflected our national aspirations for culture and our sense of inferiority as we measured ourselves against Europe.

Now, over a century later, Congress has mandated another report on the state of arts education in the United States. Insecurity about our ability to compete in world markets has reappeared; but this time Congress has made it clear that cultural, not economic, welfare is the concern:

> The Committee believes that arts and humanities education is central to the stated purpose of this Act which includes encouraging national progress and scholarship in the humanities and the arts, making citizens masters of their technology, becoming a nation which is a leader in ideas and spirit, and bringing to all our citizens a better understanding of the past and a better view of the future.

Concern about the breadth and quality of education in American schools was highlighted in the 1983 report of the National Commission on Excellence in Education, *A Nation at Risk*. Since then a rash of books and reports have publicized the erosion of education standards, the decline in test scores and, especially, the glaring lack of cultural knowledge and awareness on the part of most high school graduates. These studies agree that while time must be set aside for students to master modern skills, such as computer sciences, achievement of computer literacy must not substitute for literacy in the culture that all Americans share.

The 1987 best-seller status achieved by Allan Bloom's *The Closing of the American Mind* and E.D. Hirsch, Jr.'s *Cultural Literacy* testifies to the fact that far from being a passing fad, worry about the cultural aspects of education is growing. Increasingly, this concern is focusing on what, if anything, our children are learning about the arts and the humanities which together are at the center of culture and civilization.

Many of the conclusions in the present study echo those reached in the report of the National Endowment for the Humanities, *American Memory,* published in August 1987. We strongly endorse the Humanities

Endowment's condemnation of teaching that emphasizes narrow skills at the expense of content and understanding; we agree that the teaching of literature has deteriorated sharply since its subsumption under the so-called "language arts"; and we strongly support the Humanities Endowment's plea for increasing the hours devoted to history, the only discipline through which our children can gain both a sense of kinship with the great thinkers and doers of the past, and a foundation from which to transmit their own culture to future generations.

Isaac Clarke's first report to Congress comprised seven volumes. They were filled with legislative actions, school-committee records and reports, interviews with officials, local histories, speeches, and statistics. This report is only one volume, but it will attempt to capture the essence of the problem and point to practical ways in which it might be addressed.

Written to fulfill the congressional mandate, this report is also intended as an open letter to the American people, to the education community, to those who love the arts and understand their importance in education. For it is in the people's hands that the future of arts education rests.

A WORD ON SOURCES

This report relies heavily on two recent surveys conducted with the support of the U.S. Department of Education: one at the state level and one at the school district level. The 1985 *Arts, Education and the States* report sets out the findings of a 1984 survey of state education agencies undertaken by the Council of Chief State School Officers. (The survey was jointly sponsored by the Rockefeller Foundation, the U.S. Department of Education and the National Endowment for the Arts.) The 1988 "Public School District Policies and Practices in Selected Aspects of Arts and Humanities Instruction" report sets out the findings of a 1987 survey of a national probability sample of 700 school districts. This survey was undertaken especially for this report to Congress as a joint project by the U.S. Department of Education, which funded it, in collaboration with the National Endowment for the Humanities and the National Endowment for the Arts.

As directed by Congress, this report contains a synthesis of the information and insights contained in previous studies. It includes, among other things, review of 3,000 Educational Resource Information Center (ERIC) abstracts on arts education; the 1985 report by the Music Educators National Conference, *Arts in Schools: State by State;* the 1986 report by Mills and Thomson for the National Art Education Association, *A National Survey of Art(s) Education, 1984-85: A National Report on the State of the Arts in the States;* John Goodlad's *A Place Called School* (1984); Laura Chapman's *Instant Art, Instant Culture: The*

Unspoken Policy for American Schools (1982); Ernest Boyer's *High School* (1983); Theodore Sizer's *Horace's Compromise* (1984); *A Nation Prepared: Teachers for the 21st Century* (1986), from the Carnegie Forum on Education and the Economy; *Time for Results: The Governor's 1991 Report on Education* (1986); the 1984 Rand Corporation report by Day et al.; *Art History, Art Criticism, and Art Production: An Examination of Art Education in Selected School Districts* (prepared for the Getty Center for Education in the Arts); and the National Assessment of Educational Progress first and second assessments of art and music (1974 and 1981) and the writing assessment (1986).

We also reviewed arts curriculum guides from states and local school districts, books relating to education in the various arts, textbooks used by children for arts instruction, and textbooks used for the education of arts teachers. Interviews were conducted with education authorities, members of state and local arts agencies, representatives of professional associations, representatives of arts advocacy groups, teachers, supervisors, school administrators, publishers, testmakers, and members of the public.

ACKNOWLEDGMENTS

The study was undertaken in cooperation with the U.S. Department of Education and in consultation with the Committee on Labor and Human Resources of the Senate and the Committee on Education and Labor of the House of Representatives. Many people have contributed to this report. We sought information, advice, and assistance from educators, artists, academics, professional associations, arts organizations, state and local agencies, and others. Many invested considerable time in helping us. We are grateful to all of them.

We are particularly grateful to Representative Pat Williams, Chairman of the House Subcommittee on Postsecondary Education, whose deep concern for the quality and availability of arts education has contributed much to our efforts in this area. We are grateful to Representative E. Thomas Coleman and Representative Steve Bartlett for their help and interest in this effort and to Representative James M. Jeffords for arranging hearings on this subject in 1984. We are also grateful to Senators Claiborne Pell and Robert T. Stafford for their leadership in our reauthorization and for the leadership and support in this area of our appropriations committees who have approved funding for arts education over the years, in particular Representatives Sidney R. Yates and Ralph Regula and Senators Robert C. Byrd and James A. McClure.

Particular thanks are due to Chester E. Finn, Jr., Assistant Secretary of Education (Office of Educational Research and Improvement) and Counselor to the Secretary of Education, and his staff, for their invaluable assistance.

We also wish to extend heartfelt thanks to Professor Brent Wilson of Pennsylvania State University, who contributed so much to drafting this report; to Kate L. Moore, Jeanne C. Rhinelander, and Ruth Berenson of the Endowment's executive staff; and to Warren Bennett Newman, Director of the Endowment's Arts in Education Program. Their contributions have been indispensable to the compilation of this document.

Finally, we are especially indebted to the members of the National Council on the Arts and the Endowment's Advisory Committee, organized specifically to guide preparation of this report. Council and committee members were consulted throughout the study process and provided invaluable advice. Representing a variety of artistic disciplines and points of view about arts education, committee members contributed immeasurably not only to the planning of this report but to its contents. At the same time, the final contents of the report, including any deficiencies or errors, are the responsibility of the Endowment.

Parthenon, Athens, courtesy of the Greek National Tourist Organization

NATIONAL COUNCIL ON THE ARTS

Frank Hodsoll	Chairman
David N. Baker	Jazz Artist, Composer, Chairman of the Jazz Department, Indiana University, Bloomington, Indiana.
Phyllis Berney	Arts Patron, Trustee, Former Member, Wisconsin Arts Board, Eau Claire, Wisconsin.
Sally Brayley Bliss	Former Dancer and Artistic Director, Joffrey II Dancers, Trustee, Oyster Bay, New York.
Nina Brock	Former Chairman, Tennessee Arts Commission, Lookout Mountain, Tennessee.
C. Douglas Dillon	Art Collector and Patron, Former Chairman, Metropolitan Museum of Art, Former Secretary of the Treasury, Trustee, New York, New York.
Allen Drury	Novelist, Tiburon, California.
Joseph Epstein	Writer, Critic, Editor, *American Scholar*, Evanston, Illinois.
Helen Frankenthaler	Painter, New York, New York.
Robert Garfias	Ethnomusicologist, Dean of Fine Arts, University of California at Irvine, Irvine, California.
Margaret Hillis	Director, Chicago Symphony Chorus, Chicago, Illinois.
Celeste Holm	Actress, New York, New York.
Bob Johnson	State Senator, Former Chairman, Florida Arts Council, Sarasota, Florida.
M. Ray Kingston	Architect, Former Chairman, Utah Arts Council, Salt Lake City, Utah.
Ardis Krainik	General Manager, Lyric Opera of Chicago, Chicago, Illinois.
Raymond J. Learsy	Art Collector, Former Publisher, Trustee, Whitney Museum of American Art, New York, New York.
Harvey Lichtenstein	President and Executive Producer, Brooklyn Academy of Music, Brooklyn, New York.

Samuel Lipman — Music Critic, Publisher, *New Criterion,* Artistic Director, Waterloo Music Festival, New York, New York.

Talbot MacCarthy — Trustee and Former Chairman, Missouri State Council on the Arts, St. Louis, Missouri.

Arthur Mitchell — Choreographer, Executive/Artistic Director, Dance Theatre of Harlem, Former Dancer, New York City Ballet, New York, New York.

Carlos Moseley — Former President and Chairman, New York Philharmonic, Spartanburg, South Carolina.

Jacob Neusner — Writer, Ungerleider Distinguished Scholar of Judaic Studies, Brown University, Providence, Rhode Island.

Lloyd Richards — Artistic Director, Yale Repertory Theatre, Producer, Dean, Yale School of Drama, New Haven, Connecticut.

George Schaefer — Theater, Film and Television Director, Dean, UCLA's Theater Arts, Film and Television Department, Los Angeles, California.

Robert Stack — Actor, Los Angeles, California.

William L. Van Alen — Architect, Wilmington, Delaware.

James Wood — Director, Art Institute of Chicago, Chicago, Illinois.

MEMBERS OF THE ADVISORY COMMITTEE

Gordon M. Ambach — Executive Director, Council of Chief State School Officers, Washington, D.C. Former New York Commissioner of Education.

Maya Angelou — Author, actress, composer, Winston-Salem, North Carolina. Reynold Professor of American Studies, Wake Forest University.

Christopher Van Antwerp — Executive Director, Michigan Association of Community Arts Agencies, Grand Rapids, Michigan.

Leonard Bernstein — Conductor, composer, former Music Director, New York Philharmonic, New York, New York.

James F. Boesen — Principal, Apple Valley High School, Apple Valley, Minnesota. 1986 Kennedy Center Arts Alliance Awardee.

Ernest L. Boyer — President, Carnegie Foundation for the Advancement of Teaching, Princeton, New Jersey. Former U. S. Commissioner of Education.

J. Carter Brown — Director, National Gallery of Art, Washington, D.C.

Raymond W. Campeau — Visual Arts Teacher, Bozeman High School, Bozeman, Montana. Recipient of 1987 Governor's Award of the Arts.

Laura H. Chapman — Consultant, author of *Instant Art, Instant Culture: The Unspoken Policy For American Schools,* Cincinnati, Ohio.

Nancy S. Cole — Dean of the College of Education at the University of Illinois at Urbana-Champaign, Illinois. President, American Educational Research Association (AERA).

Brazeal W. Dennard — Supervisor of Music in Detroit Public Schools, Director of the Brazeal Dennard Chorale, Detroit, Michigan.

Stephen Donadio — Chairman, Department of American Literature and Civilization, Middlebury College, Middlebury, Vermont.

Leilani Lattin Duke — Director, The Getty Center for Education in the Arts, Los Angeles, California.

Elliot Eisner — Professor of Education and Art, Author, Stanford University, Stanford, California.

Frank Owen Gehry — Architect, Venice, California. Worked with elementary school programs, taught at Yale Architecture School and Harvard Graduate School of Design.

Robert Glidden — Dean, School of Music, Florida State University, Talahassee, Florida. President, National Association of Schools of Music.

Kay H. Goodwin — Arts education consultant, former Chairman, West Virginia Arts and Humanities Commission, Ripley, West Virginia.

Sam W. Grabarski — Executive Director, Minnesota State Arts Board, St. Paul, Minnesota.

Harriet Keyserling	Member of South Carolina House of Representatives and Chairman of Joint Legislative Committee on Cultural Affairs, Beaufort, South Carolina.
Robert Lee Kidd III	Music teacher, Eisenhower Elementary School, Norman, Oklahoma.
Wayne Lawson	Executive Director, Ohio Arts Council, Columbus, Ohio. Former Chairman, National Assembly of State Arts Agencies.
Fred Lazarus IV	President, The Maryland Institute, College of Art, Baltimore, Maryland.
Paul Lehman	Professor of Music Education and Associate Dean, University of Michigan, Ann Arbor, Michigan. Former President, Music Educators National Conference.
Stanley Madeja	Dean, College of Visual and Performing Arts, Northern Illinois University, DeKalb, Illinois.
Bruce Marks	Artistic Director, Boston Ballet, Boston, Massachusetts. Board Member, American Council for the Arts.
Judith F. Melillo	Music teacher, Conant Elementary School, Acton, Massachusetts. President, Massachusetts Music Educators Association.
Charles A. Qualley	President, National Art Education Association and Area Coordinator for Art Education, Department of Fine Arts, University of Colorado-Boulder, Boulder, Colorado.
Thomas A. Shannon	Executive Director, National School Boards Association, Alexandria, Virginia.
Barbara Salisbury Wills	Associate Professor, Department of Drama, The University of Texas at Austin, Austin, Texas. Textbook author and President of American Association of Theatre for Youth.

Head of an Oba, National Museum of African Art, Smithsonian Institution, Eliot Elisofon Archives, Washington

Excerpts from The National Foundation on the Arts and the Humanities Act of 1965, as Amended (20 U.S.C. 951 et seq.)

Sec. 10 (e)(1) The Chairperson of the National Endowment for the Arts and the Chairperson of the National Endowment for the Humanities, with the cooperation of the Secretary of Education, shall conduct jointly a study of —

(A) the state of arts education and humanities education, as currently taught in the public elementary and secondary schools in the United States; and

(B) the current and future availability of qualified instructional personnel, and other factors, affecting the quality of education in the arts and humanities in such schools.

(2) The Endowments shall consult with the Committee on Labor and Human Resources of the Senate and the Committee on Education and Labor of the House of Representatives in the design and the implementation of the study required by this subsection.

(3) Not later than two years after the date of the enactment of the Arts, Humanities, and Museums Amendments of 1985, the Endowments shall submit to the President, the Congress and the States a report containing —

(A) the findings of the study under paragraph (1);

(B) the Endowments' views of the role of the arts and humanities in elementary and secondary education;

(C) recommendations designed to encourage making arts and humanities education available throughout elementary and secondary schools;

(D) recommendations for the participation by the National Endowment for the Arts and the National Endowment for the Humanities in arts education and humanities education in such schools; and

(E) an evaluation of existing policies of the National Endowment for the Arts and the National Endowment for Humanities that expressly or inherently affect the Endowments' abilities to expand such participation.

House Report 99-274 (99th Cong. 1st Sess.) Language Regarding Arts and Humanities Education

The Committee commends the initiatives undertaken by both Endowments with respect to arts and humanities education and urges both Chairpersons of the Endowments to expand upon their efforts in these areas. The National Endowment for the Humanities' support of seminars and institutes for high school and college teachers has made available at modest cost important regenerative training for thousands of teachers. In addition, its effort to encourage colleges and universities to undertake curriculum reform, particularly of general education and degree requirements, and to emphasize the central disciplines of the humanities has had rapid and direct effects on many colleges and universities. The Committee encourages the Endowment for the Humanities to continue these efforts. Additionally, the Committee believes the issue of the condition of arts and humanities education should receive particular study.

The Committee believes that arts and humanities education is central to the stated purpose of this Act which includes encouraging national progress and scholarship in the humanities and the arts, making citizens masters of their technology, becoming a nation which is a leader in ideas and spirit, and bringing to all our citizens a better understanding of the past and a better view of the future. The Committee also recognizes that arts and humanities education play an important role in cognitive learning and in making the arts and humanities less elitist and more available to all citizens.

In Section 102 of the bill the Committee includes in the Preamble an elaboration of the role of the Endowments in arts and humanities education in the schools to enable students to recognize and appreciate the aesthetic dimensions of our lives, artistic and scholarly expression, and the diversity of excellence that comprises our cultural heritage.

In Section 105 of the bill, the Committee further clarifies by adding a provision to section 5(c), that the National Endowment for the Arts is authorized to fund projects and productions that will encourage public knowledge, understanding and appreciation of the arts.

The Committee incorporates this provision in section 5(c) to emphasize its belief that federal support for the arts should reflect a charge to NEA to fund activities and individuals for purposes which educate as well as entertain the public about the arts. The Committee believes that this addition to section 5(c) complements the other provisions in the section and strengthens the addition of the same theme to the Declaration of Purpose in the Act, encouraging arts education for the public in the broadest sense. The addition to section 5(c) should not be construed to lessen or alter the importance of the other responsibilities delineated in the section.

Finally, in Section 110 of the bill, the Committee requires that the

Chairpersons of the National Endowments jointly, with the cooperation of the Secretary of Education, conduct a study of the state of arts and humanities education, as currently taught in the public elementary and secondary schools in the United States.

The study must examine the current and future availability of qualified instructional personnel and other factors affecting the quality of education in the arts and humanities in public elementary and secondary schools. The Endowments must consult with the Committee on Labor and Human Resources of the Senate and the Committee on Education and Labor of the House of Representatives on the design and implementation of the study.

Not later than two years after the enactment of this bill the Chairpersons of the Endowments must submit to the President, the Congress, and the States a report of the findings of this study, recommendations for encouraging arts and humanities education, and recommendations for expanding the participation of the Endowments in public elementary and secondary education.

In addition, the study must assess the impact of the Endowments' policies on their participation in arts and humanities education. It must also assess whether any polices have positive or unintentional adverse effects on the Endowments' abilities to expand their support for and participation in promoting arts and humanities education in the public elementary and secondary schools.

Several excellent reports on arts in education in the schools by the Getty Foundation, the Chief State School Officers, the National Center for Education Statistics, the Endowments and others have been issued recently. It is the intent of the Committee that the Endowments use the information and findings in these studies as a primary resource for their own assessment of arts and humanities education.

Overview

In 1985, the Congress called for a "study of the state of arts education and humanities education." The National Endowment for the Humanities published its report, *American Memory*, on August 31, 1987. What follows is the report of the National Endowment for the Arts on its study of the state of arts education, the second such report in U.S. history.

WHAT IS BASIC ARTS EDUCATION?

Basic arts education aims to provide *all* students, not only the gifted and talented, with knowledge of, and skills in, the arts. Basic arts education must give students the essence of our civilization, the civilizations which have contributed to ours, and the more distant civilizations which enrich world civilization as a whole. It must also give students tools for creating, for communicating and understanding others' communications, and for making informed and critical choices.

Basic arts education includes the disciplines of literature (from the art of writing); visual art and design (from the arts of painting, sculpture, photography, video, crafts, architecture, landscape and interior design, product and graphic design); performing art (from the arts of dance, music, opera, and musical theater and theater); and media art (from the arts of film, television, and radio).

"Art, no less than philosophy or science, issues a challenge to the intellect. The great works of music, sculpture, painting, engraving, and all other forms of artistic expression engage the mind, teaching lessons about order, proportion, and genius."
—WILLIAM J. BENNETT
U.S. Secretary of Education

While each of these art disciplines differs in character, tradition, and form, basic arts education must also include art forms that are interdisciplinary: opera and musical theater, which combine vocal and instrumental music with drama and stage design; film and television, which combine music, drama, and the visual arts, synthesized by the media arts themselves; and new work that extends the frontiers of current artistic convention. Just as artists collaborate to produce interdisciplinary arts, so school faculties will need to collaborate to teach them.

Like other school subjects, basic arts education must be taught sequentially by qualified teachers; instruction must include the history, critical theory, and ideas of the arts as well as creation, production, and performance; and knowledge of, and skills in, the arts must be tested. As for other school subjects, appropriate resources—classroom time, administrative support, and textbooks—must be provided to this end.

The problem is: basic arts education does not exist in the United States today.

WHY IS BASIC ARTS EDUCATION IMPORTANT?

Our last seven Presidents have all affirmed the idea that the arts are at the core of what we are and, therefore, of what we should know. President Reagan, after quoting John Adams to the effect that his grandchildren should have "a right to study painting, poetry, music, architecture," urged us to "resolve that our schools will teach our children the same respect and

"Art is humanity's most essential, most universal language. It is not a frill, but a necessary part of communication. The quality of civilization can be measured through its music, dance, drama, architecture, visual art and literature. We must give our children knowledge and understanding of civilization's most profound works."

—ERNEST L. BOYER
President
Carnegie Foundation for the Advancement of Teaching

appreciation for the arts and humanities that the Founders had."

A balanced education is essential to an enlightened citizenry and a productive work force, and a balanced education must include comprehensive and sequential study in the three great branches of learning—the arts, humanities, and sciences. It is basic understanding of the combination of these areas of learning that provides for what E.D. Hirsch, Jr. calls "cultural literacy."

There are four reasons why arts education is important: to understand civilization, to develop creativity, to learn the tools of communication, and to develop the capacity for making wise choices among the products of the arts. Lest it be feared that arts education might detract from basic skills thought to be essential to productivity, the example of Japan, whose productivity is without question, is instructive; the Japanese require extensive and sequential arts instruction from kindergarten through twelfth grade.

Very important, arts education is essential for *all* students, not just the gifted and talented. The schools teach reading and writing (including literature) to all students, not just those who are good at these subjects. Just as knowledge of, and skills in, words are essential to functioning in society, so knowledge of, and skills in, nonverbal communication are essential. In order to cope with a 21st century permeated by technological change and the electronic media, young Americans need a sense of themselves and their civilization and of the vocabularies of the images on television. Today's kindergartners will be the first graduating class of the 21st century.

Civilization

The first purpose of arts education is to give our young people a sense of civilization. American civilization includes many cultures—from Europe, Africa, the Far East and our own hemisphere. The great works of art of these parent civilizations, and of our own, provide the guideposts to cultural literacy. Knowing them, our young people will be better able to understand, and therefore build on, the achievements of the past; they will also be better able to understand themselves. Great works of art illuminate the constancy of the human condition.

"This moment of mounting concern about American education is the time to help our dedicated teachers and our schools transmit the significance and common heritage of the arts, so that our young people will not be denied the opportunity to become citizens this Nation deserves."

—J. CARTER BROWN
Director
National Gallery of Art

Mere exposure to the best of the arts is not enough. As Elliot Eisner of Stanford University has said, the best of art needs to be "unwrapped," to be studied in order to be understood. The schools already teach the vocabularies and ideas of good writing by including great literature in English studies. But great works of art also communicate in images, sounds, and movements. The schools need to teach the vocabularies of these images, sounds, and movements, as well as of words, if young Americans are to graduate from high school with a sense of civilization.

All we know of the earliest civilizations comes to us through the arts

—whether the paintings of the caves of Lascaux, the ancient bronzes and pottery figures of pre-Shang China, or the pyramids of Egypt. Without the epics of Homer, without the Parthenon, the whole heritage of Greek civilization would be lost to us; without the bronze sculptures of Benin we would know nothing of the great African empire that antedated Spain's by nearly 100 years; without the great temples overgrown by the jungles of Mexico and Central America, the achievements of the Maya would go unremembered. Without knowledge and understanding of such supreme achievements, we are "culturally illiterate."

"When members of a society wish to secure that society's rich heritage they cherish their arts and respect their artists. The esteem with which we regard the multiple cultures offered in our country enhances our possibilities for healthy survival and continued social development."
— MAYA ANGELOU
Artist

American civilization has a central core which Henry Geldzahler, the former Fine Arts Commissioner of New York City, describes as a "sleeping giant." The core includes — to name a very few — such diverse artists as Shakespeare, Lao Tse, Cervantes, Melville, and Henry James; Praxiteles, Michelangelo, Velasquez, Frank Lloyd Wright, Winslow Homer, and Jackson Pollock; Bach, Mozart, Beethoven, Aaron Copland, and Duke Ellington; George Balanchine, Martha Graham, and Katherine Dunham; Jan Peerce, Marian Anderson, and Leontyne Price; and John Huston and Katharine Hepburn. The American giant is largely European, but includes strains of Africa, Asia, and the other parts of our own hemisphere.

In designing the contents of arts education, we must set out to make this "giant" a part of the knowledge and experience of all Americans. The "giant" *is* American civilization.

Creativity

A second purpose of arts education is to foster creativity. Young people should have the opportunity to emulate master artists — to take blank sheets of paper or rolls of film or video tape and fill them, to blow a trumpet and make melodies and rhythms, to design a house or a city, and to move in dance.

To acquire the skills with which to do this requires hard work and discipline, but to use them to create a personal vision can be a joyful experience. Moreover, whether by inference from a collection of phenomena, or by creating an initial hypothesis from which deductions might flow, learning in the arts can not only develop the discipline and craft necessary to constructive creation, it can also help students to develop reasoning and problem-solving skills essential to a productive work force and to the learning of other subjects.

Trying to create or perform the nonliterary arts without skills and knowledge is like trying to write without vocabulary and syntax. The student is reduced to being the "first artist." No one would dream of teaching the art of writing that way, just as no one would teach mathematics or physics without the benefit of Euclid or Newton. Arts education must include the vocabularies and basic skills which produced the great works

MR. WILLIAM
SHAKESPEARES
COMEDIES,
HISTORIES, &
TRAGEDIES.

Publiſhed according to the True Originall Copies.

LONDON
Printed by Iſaac Iaggard, and Ed. Blount. 1623.

William Shakespeare,
Title Page of First Folio,
The Folger Shakespeare
Library, Washington

of the past so that young people can build on those who came before.

To create and perform works of art is also to engage actively in the process of worldmaking. As the well-known psychologist Jerome Bruner reminds us, Aristotle in the *Poetics* observed that "the poet's function is to describe, not the thing that has happened, but a kind of thing that might happen." Bruner notes that tyrants hate and fear poets "even more than they fear and hate scientists, who, though they create possible worlds, leave no place in them for possible alternative personal perspectives on those worlds." Such perspectives are very much the domain of the poet, the artist. The function of art is "to open us to dilemmas, to the hypothetical"; it is in this respect "an instrument of freedom, lightness, imagination, and yes, reason."

Communication

A third purpose of arts education is to teach effective communication. As great orators and writers through history have shown, speaking and writing are art forms; the best of writing becomes "literature" and is studied as such. But all writing, whether it is a political speech, advertising copy, a novel or a poem, is an attempt to communicate to readers. The other art forms also have languages through which artists speak to audiences. The language may be primarily verbal, as in literature, or nonverbal, as in music, dance, or the visual and design arts, or it may be a combination of both, as in drama, opera and musical theater, and the media arts. Young people must be given an education enabling them to understand these languages and to analyze their meanings.

Their education should include learning elementary artistic skills which can be used in later life — whether visually to express some nonverbal concept in a corporate board room, or to play a phrase on a piano to illustrate tonal differences, or to sing a song, or to use acting techniques to make a point or tell a joke effectively, or to record in words or line an especially memorable personal experience.

Understanding of nonverbal communication is especially important in a time when television has become a principal medium of communication. Television reaches everywhere. It is of prime importance in judging and electing our leaders; its dramas influence the vocabularies of our languages and reinforce or detract from our prejudices; its practitioners' names are household words; young people spend more time watching it than they spend in school. Television may well be the most important innovation in communication since the printing press, and it communicates in images that are as much visual and aural as verbal. It employs all the arts, which in turn are synthesized by the art of television itself. For students, learning the vocabularies of all the arts, including the media arts, is an essential tool for understanding, and perhaps one day communicating in the medium of television.

Television itself is also changing in ways that will make it easier to use on behalf of the arts. Broadcast is becoming less important as cable and cassette technologies, with their potential for reaching specialized audiences, penetrate the marketplace. The audience share for network television has dropped from 91 percent in 1977 to 69 percent in 1987. The newer technologies have the potential to empower audiences with special interests and those with special messages. But if this empowerment is to take place, young people must learn the vocabularies of television.

It is something of an anomaly that the schools make little effort to teach young people the rudiments of television's vocabularies. No one disputes that literature should be a basic part of English studies, if only because the best writers serve as models for students who are learning the craft of writing. While television is still a new medium and there are as yet few models that have withstood the test of time, it is curious that the schools have so far taken little or no interest in educating their students in the art and craft of making images on television.

Choice

A fourth purpose of arts education is to provide tools for critical assessment of what one reads, sees and hears. It should provide both models and standards of excellence. It should also provide a sense of the emotional power of the arts, their ability to stir an audience, both to inspire it and manipulate it. Arts education can give people the tools to make better choices and even to influence the marketplace of both products and ideas.

Every child growing up in the United States is bombarded from birth with popular art and artful communication over the airways and on the streets. The purpose of arts education is not to wean young people from these arts (an impossible task even if it were desirable) but to enable them to make reasoned choices about them and what is good and bad.

Arts education can help make discriminating consumers. Understanding the art of design, for example, can lead to better industrial products, as the Japanese understood when they swamped our automobile market. Similarly, knowledge of design enables the citizenry to make informed choices affecting where and how we live. Understanding of the media arts could affect the Nielsen and Arbitron ratings which dictate the broadcast agenda.

WHAT IS THE PROBLEM?

Several impediments stand in the way of arts education. According to a 1986 Gallup poll, Americans generally view job preparation as the principal reason for schooling, and knowledge not obviously related to job skills as relatively unimportant. Our preoccupation with the practical has made education focus on limited basic skills (reading, writing, arithmetic, and now computer literacy) while neglecting education in what those skills are to be used for. Americans also generally confuse the arts with entertainment which can be enjoyed without understanding. Some go so far as to think of the arts as potentially threatening or even blasphemous. Further, because there is little agreement on what arts education should be, there is no agreed course of action to rally those who believe in it.

To sum up, the arts are in triple jeopardy: they are not viewed as serious; knowledge itself is not viewed as a prime educational objective; and those who determine school curricula do not agree on what arts education is.

THE STATE OF ARTS EDUCATION TODAY

There is a major gap between the stated commitment and resources available to arts education and the actual practice of arts education in schools.

Arts education, generally limited to instruction in music, drawing, painting, and crafts, has always had a place, even if a minor one, in America's schools. And the current move for educational reform has to a certain extent embraced the arts as well as the sciences and humanities. Most national education authorities—Secretary of Education William Bennett, the Council of Chief State School Officers, the National School Boards Association, the National Education Association, the American Federation of Teachers, the College Board—support the general concept of making arts teaching a part of basic education.

At the state level, 29 states have enacted high school graduation requirements which in some way include the arts, 27 of them in the past eight years (see Figure 1); and 42 states require school districts to offer arts instruction in elementary, middle, or secondary school.

At the school district level, consistent with state level trends, a growing number of districts now require units in the arts for graduation from high school. The number of districts reporting increases between 1982 and 1987 in the number of arts courses being offered is greater than those reporting decreases. In addition, 50 percent of school districts report that the percentage of their budgets allocated to arts education increased during these years. While a majority of districts reported that between 1982 and 1987 the percent of classroom time in the school day for arts education stayed the same, more than a third reported that the amount of time had increased, and only 6 percent reported decreases.

Nationally, there are almost as many music and visual art teachers in the schools as science teachers. The amount of time allocated to arts instruction in grades one through six averages 12 percent of classroom time for the majority of students. This increases to 17 percent for the majority of students in grades seven and eight, and in these grades arts courses in music and the visual arts are usually taught by certified specialist teachers in these areas.

Figure 1. States with Graduation Requirements in the Arts

STATE	Number	Subject
* ARKANSAS	½	Drama, Music, Visual Arts
CALIFORNIA	1	Fine Arts (Creative Writing, Dance, Drama, Music, Visual Arts) or Foreign Language
CONNECTICUT	1	Arts (Dance, Drama, Music, Visual Arts) or Vocational Education
* FLORIDA	½	Fine Arts (Dance, Drama, Music, Visual Arts)
GEORGIA	1	Fine Arts (Dance, Drama, Music, Visual Arts), Vocational Education or Computer Technology
HAWAII	1	For academic honors only Art or Music
IDAHO	4[1]	Fine Arts (Creative Writing, Dance, Drama, Music, Visual Arts), Foreign Language or Humanities
ILLINOIS	1	Art, Music, Foreign Language or Vocational Education
INDIANA	2	For students seeking an Honors Diploma
LOUISIANA	½	For students in the Regents Program (typically, the college-bound)
MAINE	1[1]	Fine Arts (Visual Arts, Music, Drama) or Forensics
* MARYLAND	1[1]	Fine Arts (Dance, Drama, Music, Visual Arts)
* MISSOURI	1	Music or Visual Arts
* NEW HAMPSHIRE	½	Arts Education (Art, Music, Visual Arts, Dance, Drama)
NEW JERSEY	1	Fine Arts, Practical Arts or Performing Arts

NEW MEXICO	½	Fine Arts (Visual Arts, Music, Dance, Drama), Practical Arts or Vocational Education
*NEW YORK	1[2]	Dance, Drama, Music, or Visual Arts
NEVADA	1[3]	Fine Arts or Humanities
NORTH CAROLINA	1	For students enrolled in the Scholars Program
OREGON	1	Music, Visual Arts, Foreign Language or Vocational Education
PENNSYLVANIA	2	Arts (Dance, Drama, Music, Visual Arts) or Humanities
RHODE ISLAND	½	For college-bound students only. Dance, Drama, Music or Visual Arts
*SOUTH DAKOTA	½	Fine Arts (Dance, Drama, Music, Visual Arts)
TENNESSEE	2	For students seeking an Honors Diploma
TEXAS	1	For advanced academic program students only. Drama, Music or Visual Arts
*UTAH	1½	Dance, Drama, Music or Visual Arts
*VERMONT	1	General Arts, Dance, Drama, Music or Visual Arts
VIRGINIA	1[1]	Fine Arts (Art, Music, Dance, Theatre) or Practical Arts
WEST VIRGINIA	1	Music, Visual Arts or Applied Arts

*States that require some study of the arts by every high school student.

[1] Effective 1988.

[2] Effective 1989.

[3] Effective 1992.

This table is a revision of one first published in *Arts, Education and the States: A Survey of State Education Policies* (Washington, D.C.: Council of Chief State School Officers, 1985), updated with information from the National Art Education Association; Alliance for Arts Education, The John F. Kennedy Center for the Performing Arts; and the National Assembly of State Arts Agencies.

However, these developments have not resulted in basic arts education. In few if any school districts in the nation are these stated commitments and resources translated into the kind of actual teaching and learning in the arts that would give *all* students sequential opportunities to understand and contribute to their civilization, to participate in and develop a sense of the creative and problem-solving process, to communicate and understand communication in visual and aural images as well as words, and to make wise choices among the products of the arts.

Arts graduation requirements are often vague and sometimes listed as alternatives to requirements in other subject areas. Of the 29 states that require the arts for high school graduation, 13 accept courses in domestic science, industrial arts, humanities, foreign languages, or computer sciences as alternative ways of meeting them. Only nine states require arts courses per se for all students; seven more require them only for college-bound or honors-program students. Further, college-bound students have little incentive to elect arts courses in high school because many colleges will not accept them for credit.

Most elementary school classroom teachers have had little formal training in the arts. Access of elementary school students to arts specialist teachers varies widely among regions, and except in music is often lacking (see Figure 2). There are few texts and other instructional materials actually available in elementary school arts classrooms. In middle and junior high schools, specialist teachers and instructional materials in fields other than music and the visual arts are usually lacking, and even where they are present, students will learn little of the great works of art. High school courses are usually performance oriented and focused on those with special talent or interest. Practically no attention is given at any grade level to the media and design arts and dance.

Student enrollments in music and visual art courses are substantial in grades seven and eight on a national basis, on the order of half the students in those grades (see Figure 3, p. 24). However, enrollment rates in these subjects drop precipitously in grades nine to 12 (reaching a level on the order of 10 to 20 percent), and enrollments in all other arts courses are low for grades seven to 12 (on the order of 12 to 14 percent). Interestingly, rural districts have higher enrollment rates in music than suburban districts, but lower enrollments in visual arts. On a regional basis, the Northeast has generally the highest enrollments in arts courses (on the order of 80 percent for general music and visual arts in grades seven and eight) and the West the lowest enrollments (21 percent for general music and 35 percent for visual arts in grades seven and eight).

Figure 2. Percentage of Elementary Schools Served by Visual Art and Music Specialists, 1986-87, (50 States and D.C.)

NATIONAL

Visual Arts Specialists

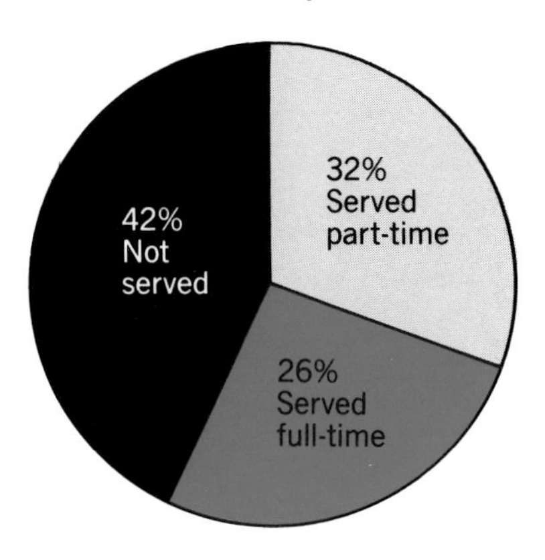

Percentage of Elementary Schools Served by Visual Arts Specialists, by Region,* 1986-87

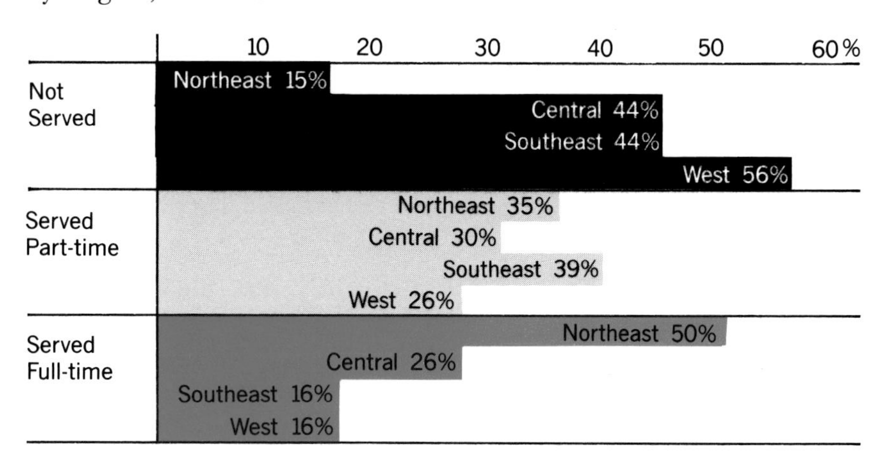

Music Specialists

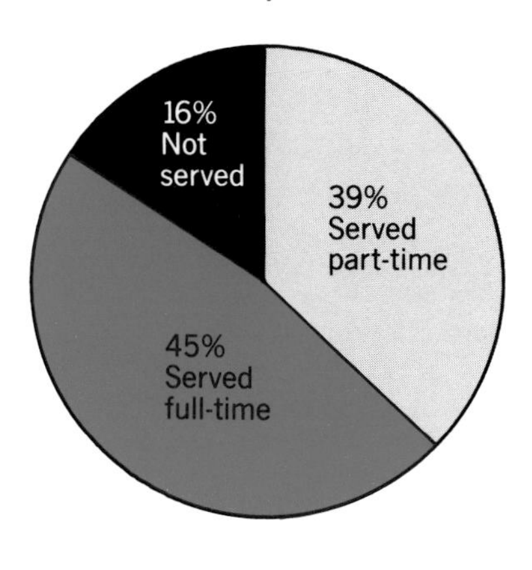

Percentage of Elementary Schools Served by Music Specialists, by Region,* 1986-87

10 20 30 40 50 60 %

Not Served
Northeast 3%
Central 19%
Southeast 20%
West 21%

Served Part-time
Northeast 37%
Central 35%
Southeast 41%
West 42%

Served Full-time
Northeast 60%
Central 46%
Southeast 39%
West 37%

Source: Center for Education Statistics, "Public School District Policies and Practices in Selected Aspects of Arts and Humanities Instruction," U.S. Department of Education Bulletin, February 1988, Figure 5, p. 10 and Table 10, p. 24.

*The **Northeast** includes districts in Connecticut, Delaware, the District of Columbia, Maine, Maryland, Massachusetts, New Hampshire, New Jersey, New York, Pennsylvania, Rhode Island, and Vermont. The **Central** region includes districts in Illinois, Indiana, Iowa, Kansas, Michigan, Minnesota, Missouri, Nebraska, North Dakota, Ohio, South Dakota, and Wisconsin. The **Southeast** includes districts in Alabama, Arkansas, Florida, Georgia, Kentucky, Louisiana, Mississippi, North Carolina, South Carolina, Tennessee, Virginia, and West Virginia. The **West** includes districts in Alaska, Arizona, California, Colorado, Hawaii, Idaho, Montana, Nevada, New Mexico, Oklahoma, Oregon, Texas, Utah, Washington, and Wyoming.

Figure 3. Student Enrollments in the Arts, Grades 7-12, 1986-87 by National, Regional & Metropolitan Status (50 States and D.C.)

Subject and grade	Average percentage of students enrolled or participating							
		Geographic region				Metropolitan status		
	All districts	North-east	Central	South-east	West	Urban	Sub-urban	Rural
Music (general)								
Grades 7-8	48	81	51	45	21	54	42	52
Grades 9-10	12	21	13	9	7	13	8	17
Grades 11-12	9	15	11	7	5	9	7	13
Instrumental music								
Grades 7-8	23	22	27	17	23	21	23	24
Grades 9-10	16	14	21	13	14	13	15	18
Grades 11-12	14	12	19	12	12	11	14	16
Choral music								
Grades 7-8	23	27	30	16	16	17	22	26
Grades 9-10	13	13	19	9	9	9	12	15
Grades 11-12	12	11	17	9	7	8	12	13
Visual arts								
Grades 7-8	53	79	59	42	35	58	52	51
Grades 9-10	21	28	24	14	16	22	22	17
Grades 11-12	16	18	21	13	14	15	19	13
Other arts								
Grades 7-8	14	12	17	9	15	14	14	13
Grades 9-10	12	10	15	10	13	12	12	12
Grades 11-12	13	12	16	10	11	12	13	12

Source: Center for Education Statistics, "Public School District Policies and Practices in Selected Aspects of Arts and Humanities Instruction," U.S. Department of Education Bulletin, February 1988, Tables 8 and 9, pp. 22-23. For a regional listing of states, see Figure 2.

Our only sense of student achievement in, and knowledge of the arts comes from the National Assessment of Educational Progress, which twice in the 1970's assessed student abilities in the visual arts and music. The results were not encouraging. The Assessment reported that in 1979 high school students knew less about music than their peers knew in 1971. In the visual arts, test performances also declined. There is little reason to believe that the situation has changed for the better.

The artistic heritage that is ours and the opportunities to contribute significantly to its evolution are being lost to our young people. In 1982, and again in 1985, we learned that 61 percent of American adults had not attended even once in the previous 12 months a single live performance of jazz, classical music, opera, musical theater, or ballet; nor had they visited a museum or art gallery. That 39 percent of adult Americans — over 65 million citizens — did participate in these arts is likely an enormous improvement over, say, 20 years ago, but the fact remains that the cultural heritage and most contemporary expression outside the popular culture of the moment are not part of the lives of most Americans. There is evidence that arts education can make a difference.

Curriculum

What should teachers teach in the arts? There is little agreement about the content of arts education: what should be required, what should be taught separately, what should be integrated into the teaching of other subjects. Nor is there any consensus in arts education about the relative emphasis that should be placed on teaching history, skills, and critical judgment.

There is equal confusion about learning goals, how much students can absorb and at what grade levels. There is a consensus that the arts should be taught sequentially, and certain professional associations of arts educators have agreed on comprehensive curricula for their disciplines. However, there is little or no agreement among state and local education agencies about how the variety of the arts should be taught. In short, educational decision makers are bewildered by the question: what should every high school graduate, whether college bound or entering the work force, know about the arts?

In most states, curriculum guides are available to local districts. But these guides vary from state to state, and tend to emphasize narrowly focused skill outcomes at the expense of the art form as a whole and of the cultural significance of great works of art. Because many teachers lack a background in teaching the great works of art, they are unable to overcome this deficiency. Further, the guides tend to replicate existing guides and ignore the best theoretical work available; they also often fail at the elementary school level to provide nonspecialists with the practical information they need for classroom instruction.

Two-thirds to three-quarters of school districts provide curriculum guides for music and the visual arts; but only about one-third have them for dance, theater, and creative writing. There are virtually none for the arts of design — architecture, urban planning, historic preservation, product and graphic design—although these arts more intimately affect our lives than any except the media arts, for which curriculum guides are also unavailable. Even in music, half the school districts do not have recommended or required textbooks, a situation much worse in the other arts.

Secretary of Education William Bennett proposed in December 1987 a model high school curriculum, the graduation requirements of which included a minimum of one semester each in art history and music history. It is the conclusion of the present report that the minimum high school requirement should be two full years involving the arts, to provide *all* high school students with a basic sense of the history and vocabularies of the arts and their significance in society. It should be remembered that the arts include more than visual art and music; high school requirements should, building on the knowledge and skills learned in elementary and middle school, assure for all students basic familiarity with the contributions of all the arts as a condition of obtaining a high school diploma.

This minimum two-year requirement might be met either through arts courses per se or through making the arts integral parts of other courses. This conclusion is based on the belief that the basic learning objectives of arts education might be achieved in different ways in different schools or districts and that integration of arts components in other courses (e.g., history) might be an effective way to accomplish at least some of these objectives.

Testing and Evaluation

Schools have little or no idea what their students are learning about the arts. Nowhere in the country is there any systematic, comprehensive, and formal assessment of student achievement in the arts; nor is the effectiveness of specific arts programs in local school districts generally measured. Only about 6 percent of school districts require district-wide competency tests in the arts for promotion to the next grade.

There are three unique problems involved in arts testing. The first is the lack of standardized curricula, texts, and resource materials against which to test; the second is that the arts do not readily lend themselves to easily scorable testing formats; and the third is the dispute among arts educators about whether testing in arts education is a good idea.

Nationally, our only sense of student achievement and knowledge of the visual arts and music comes from the National Assessment of Educational Progress (NAEP), which twice in the 1970's assessed student abilities in those subjects. Although the original NAEP plan provided for a new assessment of music and visual art at least every six years, none has been conducted since 1979, and some data from the 1978-79 visual art assessment remain unreported. The Reagan administration has proposed expansion of NAEP to provide for state-by-state comparisons. If the NAEP expansion were extended to the arts, it would permit national and state-level assessment and comparisons. Testing in the arts cannot be left exclusively to the state and district levels; they need help in designing and implementing the tests. NAEP is in a unique position to do this.

The need to measure individual progress toward curricular goals and objectives and to evaluate the relative effectiveness of arts education programs is as essential as for other subjects. Without testing and evaluation, there is no way to measure individual and program progress, program objectives will lack specificity, and arts courses will continue to be considered extra-curricular and unimportant. As the Dutch experience with testing in the arts demonstrates, what is tested is what is viewed as important.

Teachers

The arts must be taught by teachers knowledgeable in them. At the elementary level, schools often have to rely on general classroom teachers to provide arts instruction; fewer than half the nation's elementary schools have access to full-time music specialists and only a quarter have access to full-time visual arts specialists (see Figure 2, p. 23). But is the general classroom teacher required to take specific courses or units in the arts in order to be certified to teach? As of 1984, in most states the answer was "no."

Arts specialists, on the other hand, usually have intensive training in their discipline and in how to teach it. Virtually all states certify specialists in visual art and music, but only 24 states certify theater teachers and only 16 certify dance teachers. We know of no state which has established teacher certification programs in the design and media arts.

Substantively, teacher preparation programs for arts specialists need to provide more emphasis on history, critical analysis, aesthetics, and the philosophy of the arts if arts education is to provide an understanding of the artistic heritage, as stipulated in most state curriculum guides. State credentialing agencies need to strengthen standards for arts teacher preparation programs and develop comprehensive examinations for teacher certification. Also, once established in their profession, arts teachers need opportunities to grow in knowledge and expertise; comprehensive, systematic programs for this are few.

Recent proposals for reform in the teaching profession—specifically those of the "Holmes Group" and the Carnegie Task Force on Teaching as a Profession—could have important implications for teachers of the arts, whether generalists, arts specialists, or teachers specializing in subjects other than the arts. The emphasis on a broad liberal arts undergraduate

Jennifer
Jon
Brando

education (with less emphasis on education courses) combined with a proposed requirement for graduate study in education methods could provide greater opportunity at the undergraduate level for substantive education in the arts for the elementary school classroom teacher. But for the arts specialist, such an approach might detract from the best preparation programs. These combine education in the art form with education in teaching methods and actual practice in classrooms, and employ professors of arts education to teach pedagogy in such a way that methods are not divorced from content.

Reform proposals also emphasize that the standing and compensation of teachers must be raised. This is especially critical in light of the prospective turnover in the teaching profession as many teachers approach retirement. Shortages of arts teachers exist even now in schools. The children of the "baby boom" generation will intensify the demand for more teachers, including arts teachers. To meet these demands, more attention must be paid to improving the professional environment for teachers so as to encourage new entrants into the teaching force. Consideration also needs to be given to encouraging and credentialing qualified practicing artists and arts professionals to supplement arts teachers, particularly where shortages exist.

Research

Although most arts education research is conducted by college and university professors who must personally subsidize their own efforts, American researchers continue to produce a small but vital body of research that surpasses that of other countries in volume and quality. Unfortunately, most of this research is confined to the visual arts and music and fails to reach teachers in schools.

Baseline and trend data are lacking on the goals and objectives of arts education programs, enrollment in such programs, staffing patterns, and instructional and assessment practices. There is also a severe lack of research about how young people learn about the arts and what they can be expected to learn at what ages. The federally sponsored Educational Research Information Center (ERIC) regularly publishes abstracts on education, but is incomplete in its coverage of arts education.

The Arts Endowment, working with the U.S. Department of Education, is attempting a modest remedy here. The two agencies have collaborated in developing state and school-district-level data, and in September 1987 established research centers for arts and literature education. It is hoped that these centers, together with an Elementary Subjects Center (which includes the arts), will provide a national resource for educational decision makers and arts education professionals.

Leadership

The arts are taught in schools because concerned citizens value them. If they are to be taught well, they must have the support of all four sectors that affect arts education: the governance, education, arts, and business-producer sectors. The governance sector, which includes elected and appointed government officials as well as parents and the voters, sets the societal goals to be achieved by education. The education sector, which includes education agencies, administrators, teachers, and professional associations, implements educational programs. The arts sector creates, produces, presents, exhibits, and preserves the arts. The business-producer sector produces materials, supplies, and equipment for use in schools.

To make arts education an educational priority and a part of general education reform in the United States requires leadership from individuals and organizations in each of the four sectors. To do this, they must (i) have a consensus on the nature of arts education and how it can be accomplished, (ii) understand the factors that will lead to change, and (iii) work together to effect that change. Individuals and organizations within each of the four sectors must transcend their special interests and work together if arts education is to become a basic and sequential part of the curriculum.

All members of the education sector must understand that providing basic arts education is a fundamental part of their responsibility, and thus in their professional interest to implement. The arts can only become integrated into the basic curriculum through the efforts of the education sector. However, the advocacy of arts education programs cannot just be left to the arts educators alone, for they lack the clout by themselves to make the arts a national priority. Initiatives from outside the education sector need to be coordinated with state and locally mandated school programs.

Within the education sector, leadership in schools and school districts is most important. While the efforts of the arts teachers are of the highest importance, leadership of school and school district administrators (principals and superintendents) and of school boards is equally essential. Where this leadership is present, the arts can become a basic and the schools can make a difference; where it is not, they cannot. In exercising this leadership, school administrators must have as high expectations for arts education and provide for as frequent assessment of student progress as they do for other basic subjects.

Arts education has high standing in principle in the governance sector. Presidents of the United States, from George Washington on, have affirmed the importance of the arts. Congress is similarly on record, changing the purposes of the enabling legislation of the National Endowment for the Arts and requesting this report. So are state legislatures, as evidenced by the enactment of new graduation requirements in the arts by some states and in the 1983 resolution of the National Conference of State Legislatures. The National Congress of Parents and Teachers (the National PTA) has stated that the integration of the arts in the elementary, secondary, and continuing education curriculum is a "goal of the highest priority."

In the education sector, the National School Boards Association, the Council of Chief State School Officers, the Board of the Association for Supervision and Curriculum Development, the American Federation of Teachers, the National Education Association, and the College Board have all called for making the arts a more basic and sequential part of K-12 education. Of particular interest is the 1988 resolution of the Executive Council of the American Federation of Teachers:

> The basic school curriculum, K-12, as a part of a balanced course of study in the arts, sciences and humanities, should require all students to study the arts. Students should be required to study the literary arts; the visual arts including design and architecture; the performing arts including music, dance, opera and theater; and the media arts in order to ensure that all students will be able to develop their creative potential and graduate from high school with a basic understanding of their society and of civilization.

The U.S. Department of Education and Secretary William Bennett have shown particular commitment to arts education as a basic. In his 1986 report on elementary education, *First Lessons,* Secretary Bennett declared that the "arts are an essential element of education just like reading, writing and arithmetic." His 1987 booklet containing suggestions for a core curriculum for American high school students, *James Madison High School: A Curriculum for American Students,* recommended one semester each in art history and music history. Secretary Bennett has also spoken out on behalf of arts education on several occasions.

The arts sector has always had a major interest in arts education, although its primary efforts appropriately involve artistic creation, production, presentation, exhibition, and preservation. Both artists and arts institutions have, nonetheless, undertaken extensive and important programs of educational value. The commercial media of television, radio, the movies, recording, and publishing are most pervasive; young people spend more time in front of the television set than in school, and the popular culture is a part of the basic vocabulary of all young people.

State and local arts agencies, in addition to the National Endowment for the Arts, assist arts education in schools in their states and localities, primarily through funding, with Endowment help, artist residencies. Arts sector advocates and trustees of arts institutions can be a major force on behalf of arts education, in some cases the only force. But, to be more effective, they need to mesh their efforts more closely with those in the education sector who have the responsibility to implement education programs.

The business-producer sector needs to be encouraged to do more for arts education. Of particular importance are the textbooks and audio-visual materials without which teachers cannot teach. Ways need to be found to induce this sector to produce and market these materials in areas presently lacking them. Today, only in music does one find complete sets of such materials.

The Endowment

The National Endowment for the Arts is to arts education what the National Endowment for the Humanities and the National Science Foundation are to humanities and science education. The Arts Endowment has from its inception assisted arts education, primarily through its Arts in Education Program. Until recently, the program concentrated on funding state arts agencies to place artists in residence in schools and other educational settings.

In addition, many of the Endowment's discipline programs have funded arts institutions to undertake educational projects of various kinds. While the Endowment's Challenge Program has in the past occasionally funded educational institutions, it was changed in 1987, in part so as to target assistance to projects which could develop "deeper and broader education in and appreciation of the arts."

In 1986, based on recommendations of the National Council on the Arts and following extensive field consultations, the Endowment shifted the thrust of its Arts in Education Program towards encouraging collaboration between state arts agencies and state education agencies in order to convince the education sector that it was its responsibility and in its interest to make the arts a basic and sequential part of K-12 education.

This shift was occasioned by Congress's making arts education a principal purpose of the Endowment's enabling legislation and by the Endowment's discovery, in its 1982 Public Participation in the Arts survey, that 61 percent of adult Americans were not participating in many of the arts the Endowment supports. It is the view of the Endowment and of the National Council on the Arts that one vital function of federal support of the arts is to help all Americans become familiar with and understand the great variety of art that lies outside the popular culture of the moment. The key to this is learning about the arts.

Notwithstanding the Endowment's increased emphasis on arts education, it spends less time and money, as a proportion of its overall activities, on arts education than do its counterpart agencies, the National

Endowment for the Humanities and the National Science Foundation, on humanities and science education. The Arts Endowment spends 3.3 percent of its current budget for its Arts in Education Program, compared to 12.8 percent of the Humanities Endowment's budget for humanities education and just over 5 percent of the Science Foundation's much larger budget for science education.

These differences derive from the fact that the Arts Endowment has traditionally focused its support on professional artists and arts institutions rather than education while the Humanities Endowment and the National Science Foundation have, from their beginnings, considered education to be one of their principal priorities. These differences may stem in part from the general perception that education in the humanities and sciences is necessary to understand, appreciate and use them, while the "serious" arts, like entertainment, can be experienced without knowing anything about them.

Any effort to make the arts a sequential part of basic education will necessarily take considerable time. Even if every school district in the nation were to agree tomorrow that sequential courses in the arts are essential to a proper education, it would be 13 years before the first student had completed a K-12 curriculum.

CONCLUSION

The results of years of neglect in arts education are evident in what adults say about their experiences in it. According to the Endowment's 1985 Survey of Public Participation in the Arts, most Americans say they have never had any form of arts instruction at all: 53 percent said "no" when asked if they had lessons or classes in music; 75 percent said "no" to lessons in the visual arts; 84 percent said "no" to lessons in ballet; 82 percent said "no" to lessons in creative writing. Eighty-four percent said they had never studied visual art appreciation; 80 percent said they had never studied music appreciation. Any instruction in music or the visual arts was likely to have occurred between the ages of 12 and 17, and music or visual arts appreciation courses were likely to have been taken only in college. This, of course, works to the disadvantage of those lacking higher education (see Figure 4).

Young people missing out on arts education not only fail to become culturally literate, they miss the joy and excitement of learning the skills of creation and problem solving in the arts. They learn neither how to communicate their thoughts and dreams nor how to interpret the communication of the thoughts and dreams of others. They miss out on learning the tools to discriminate and to make reasoned choices among the products of the arts. As John Adams, our second President, wrote to his wife, Abigail, young Americans have "a right" to this. They should not miss out.

In our pluralistic society, arts education can—and should—encompass many techniques, many activities, many disciplines. It is the responsibility of state and local education authorities to develop and establish their own definitions. But they owe it to young Americans to establish finite goals for student achievement, to describe and provide in a clearcut way what it takes to achieve those goals, and to ensure that progress toward them is monitored and evaluated. The recommendations which follow are to these ends.

Figure 4. Visual Art and Music Appreciation Courses Adults Polled in 1985 on Their Childhood Experiences

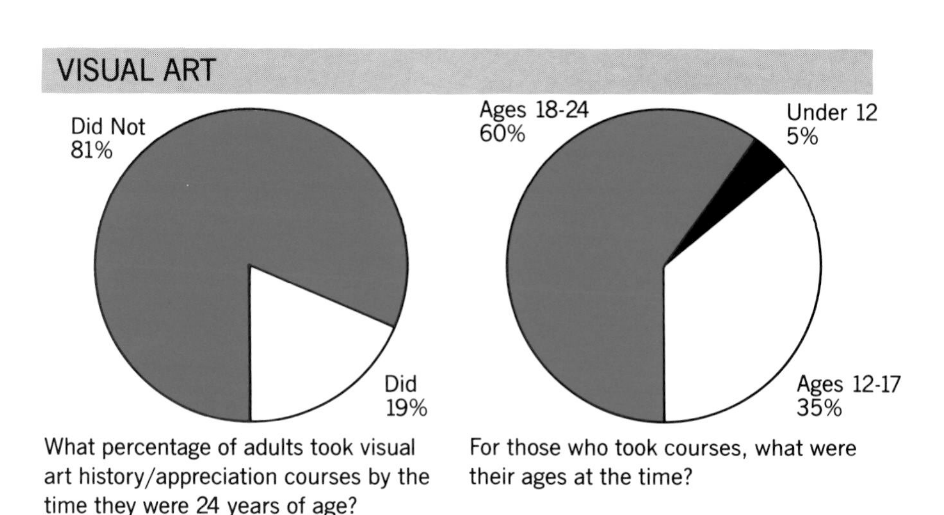

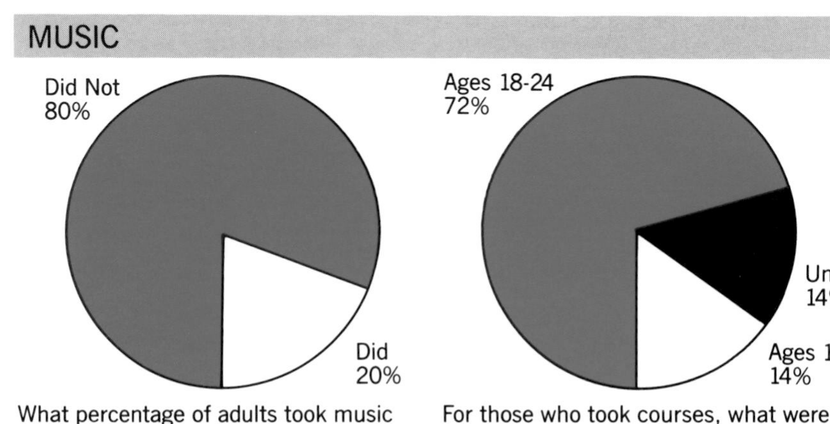

Source: Robinson, J. P., et al., "Survey of Public Participation in the Arts: 1985, Vol. 1, Project Report." December 1986, p. 371. Prepared under Cooperative Agreement NEA CA 85-24 with the National Endowment for the Arts, Washington, D.C.

RECOMMENDATIONS

Toward an Arts Curriculum

1. Arts education should provide all students with a sense of the arts in civilization, of creativity in the artistic process, of the vocabularies of artistic communication, and of the critical elements necessary to making informed choices about the products of the arts.

2. State education agencies and local school districts should adopt and implement explicit policies to make such arts education a sequential part of the basic curriculum for all students in grades K-12. These policies should define the curriculum to include each of the arts (dance, design, literature and creative writing, the media arts, music, opera and musical theater, theater, and the visual arts) and provide for instruction in history and critical analysis as well as production and performance. Most important, the policies should define a core of subject content and skills in the arts which all students would be required to achieve, and provide for a selection of required courses in relation to optional courses in the basic curriculum. It is particularly important that the policies include provision for the all-pervasive design and media arts. The policies should also provide for time, money, and qualified personnel to develop comprehensive and sequential curricula, instruction based on the curricula, and testing of student achievement and evaluation of school programs. To this end:
A. State education agencies and school districts should identify, and achieve consensus on, the minimum knowledge and skills (in terms of student learning outcomes) that would satisfy state or district-mandated high school graduation requirements.

   B. Elementary schools should consider providing arts instruction, exclusive of English studies, for approximately 15 percent of the school week consistent with the aims of professional arts education associations. Four-and-a-half hours of arts instruction in a 30-hour elementary school week is fairly minimal if students are to gain a sense of the arts as described above.

   C. Junior high and middle schools (grades 6 through 8) should require *all* students to take arts instruction, exclusive of English studies, for at least 15 percent of the school year (the average for the majority of students in grades 7 and 8 is estimated at 17 percent). These requirements might be fulfilled through survey courses, through study of at least two of the arts, or through instruction integrated with other academic courses. The curriculum should specifically require study of the design and media arts, and teachers should be trained to teach these subjects.

D. High schools should require all students satisfactorily to complete two full years (or two Carnegie units) involving the arts (not as an alternative to courses like foreign languages or computer sciences) in order to receive a graduation diploma. The purpose is to provide *all* high school students with a basic sense of the history and vocabularies of the arts and their significance in society. This purpose might be achieved either through arts courses per se or through making the arts integral parts of other courses. High schools and school systems will have to certify which of their courses meet this purpose. They may also wish to consider a seven-period day in accommodating these and other increased requirements.

E. High schools should also offer optional introductory, intermediate, and advanced courses in each of the arts so that those interested and/or talented in an art form might be able to pursue that interest and talent.

F. State education agencies and school districts should engage knowledgeable experts to coordinate arts curriculum development and evaluation. The experts should work closely with teachers and school administrators, and with theoreticians and researchers, in order to employ the best available thinking in this effort. The experts should also engage the resources of artists, arts, and cultural institutions, teacher-training institutions, and commercial producers of classroom materials.

G. State and local education budgets should provide for making appropriate arts materials (e.g., textbooks, teacher manuals, and audio-visual aids) available to students and teachers. Where such materials do not exist, state education agencies and school districts should collaborate in developing incentives for their production.

The Case for Testing and Evaluation in the Arts

1. As in other subjects, students should be tested in the arts and their art work evaluated in order to determine what they have learned, and arts education programs should be evaluated to determine their effectiveness.

2. State departments of education, local school districts and schools should identify, implement, and evaluate procedures to test student achievement and evaluate arts education programs on a comparative basis. To this end:

A. Each school district should implement a comprehensive testing program in the arts based on the district's arts curriculum. The program should address creation, performance, history, critical analysis, and the place of the arts in society, and use both quantitative and qualitative measures to determine whether the student is achieving the curriculum's learning objectives.

B. Each school district should implement an evaluation program which assesses the merit of the curriculum, adherence to it, the adequacy of resources allocated to implement it, and the level of student achievement.

C. Each state education agency should develop evaluation procedures to evaluate district and school arts programs on a comparative basis in terms of state arts education goals.

D. Each state education agency should provide technical assistance to school districts to help them develop student testing and program evaluation procedures.

3. The U.S. Department of Education and the National Endowment for the Arts should work together to restore to the National Assessment of Educational Progress assessments in visual art, music, and literature. The NAEP writing assessment should include creative writing. Before the next NAEP reauthorization, methods for assessing theater, dance, the design arts, and media arts should be developed, including development of prototype questions. Remaining data from the 1979 visual art assessment which are still unreleased should be scored, analyzed, and released as soon as possible.

Teachers of the Arts

1. **Teacher Preparation and Certification.** State certifying agencies should strengthen arts certification requirements for all teachers whose responsibilities include the arts. Training of all teachers — elementary school classroom teachers, specialist arts teachers, and teachers of other subjects to which the arts are relevant — should include (i) study of important works of art (their craft, history, and significance to the civilizations which they symbolize) and (ii) study of techniques for creating or performing one of the arts. To this end:
A. *For elementary school classroom teachers,* each state certifying agency should establish arts requirements for certification; over half of the states do not have such requirements. These requirements should include at least two courses in the arts which stress content.

B. *For K-12 arts specialists,* each state certifying agency should require training in the history and critical analysis of the art form, as well as in production and performance. Half the university course work should be in the art discipline, and methods courses in arts education should be made an integral part of substantive instruction in the arts, not separated out as recommended in the Holmes and Carnegie reports. University courses in the arts disciplines should, where relevant, draw on the standards and recommendations of the National Association of Schools of Art and

Design, the National Association of Schools of Music, the National Association of Schools of Theatre, and the National Association of Schools of Dance. Faculty responsible for teaching these courses should test their ideas about arts teaching in actual teaching situations in elementary and secondary classrooms.

C. Teacher recruitment and certification in the arts of dance, design, the media, and theater should be strengthened and instituted in those states which do not now provide for them.

D. In a time when we are likely to face a shortage of qualified arts teachers, state certifying agencies should develop and implement flexible procedures that provide for special testing and certification of experienced practicing artists and arts professionals who can demonstrate a comprehensive background in the arts and substantial knowledge of the issues and methodology of K-12 arts education.

E. *For teachers of other subjects (such as history, geography, and foreign languages)*, state certifying agencies and colleges and universities should require a basic general education in the arts. The arts are related to all school subjects, and all teachers should understand them well enough to use them to support and elucidate instruction in other subjects and to show how such subjects can contribute to an understanding of the arts.

F. Testing of teacher qualifications should be mandated as a condition of teacher certification. State certifying agencies should develop tests to evaluate teacher preparation and teacher preparation programs. Such tests should assess the general (liberal arts) preparation of teachers, their knowledge of art in the context of history and culture, their ability to analyze art, their performance and skill competencies, their knowledge of issues in arts education, and their skill in lesson planning and pedagogy.

G. Teacher preparation programs should emphasize the importance of working with local artists and arts institutions and provide information on how to draw on them.

2. **Teacher Recruitment.** Arts education professional associations, state departments of education, colleges and universities, and arts schools should undertake efforts to attract capable students to arts teacher preparation programs, including minority students. Special efforts should be made to recruit dance, design, media, and drama teachers.

3. **Teacher Professional Development.** Arts teachers, no less than teachers of other subjects, should be provided with opportunities to advance within their profession. State education agencies and school districts should develop standards and incentives to this end, and should promote career mobility within the school, district, region, or state. Such incentives should include full or partial reimbursement of expenses for summer studies and for attending professional meetings and conferences.

4. **Teaching Environment.** Local school districts should, consistent with state and local mandates, provide arts teachers with maximum flexibility to meet the individual needs of specific classes. They should also provide arts teachers with adequate compensation, facilities, administrative support, and teaching materials.

5. **Optimum Staffing.** Each school district should aim to provide arts instruction by trained arts specialists at all levels K-12. To this end:
   A. Elementary school administrators should recruit teacher curriculum coordinators for each of the arts. Where available, arts specialists should be given this responsibility; where they are not available, classroom teachers with particular interests and qualifications in the arts should serve as coordinators in the interim. Coordinators should be given time and resources and be responsible for developing sequential arts programming, for assembling necessary resources, and for assisting teachers. Professional arts education associations, artists, and arts organizations can help the coordinators in these efforts.

   B. Elementary school administrators should, especially in the upper elementary grades, assign the best arts teachers to teach the arts in several classrooms in addition to their own. In such a program, students would benefit from competent instruction and the number of subjects for which teachers would have to prepare would be reduced.

   C. In middle, junior high, and high schools, all arts classes should continue to be taught by arts specialists, or if no arts specialist is available, by qualified people in the community, including experienced artists or arts professionals.

Research Priorities in Arts Education

More sustained support is needed to improve research in arts education. Such support should help attract better graduate students, assist apprenticeships, and permit the best researchers to undertake significant long-term studies on arts education. Research priorities should be thoughtfully established by funders in consultation with arts educators in

Fred Astaire in *Top Hat*, courtesy of the American Film Institute, Washington

order (i) to improve classroom instruction and (ii) to achieve a balance between the interests of individual researchers and general research needs. To this end:

A. National, state, and local funders (public and private) should increase their priority for arts education research.

B. The U. S. Department of Education and the National Endowment for the Arts should explore ways to assure that educational statistics, surveys, and reports cover the arts with the same attention and detail as for other school subjects. One of the Educational Resource Information Centers (ERIC) should enter into the system the large backlog of documents from previously published arts education research and periodically survey current sources of information to be entered into the system in the future.

C. Reports should be generated to synthesize and disseminate the results of completed studies, to make them available to classroom teachers and serve as bases for further research.

D. Comprehensive baseline data should be collected and periodically updated to establish trend lines concerning the extent to which education programs in each of the arts are in fact established in states and school districts. These should include data on curricula and course offerings, teachers, student enrollment, materials, facilities, classroom time, budgets, administrative support, testing and evaluation techniques, and learning outcomes.

E. Research is needed to learn what kinds of teacher training, curriculum development, instructional methodology, and resources are most effective in improving arts education.

F. Research is needed to tell us what can and should be taught at what ages and how it can best be taught. Research should be included on the complete act of learning—students' interactions with teachers, the use of resources in specific classrooms, and the influence of the family and environment on learning in the arts in comparison to learning in other subjects. Research is needed to provide more information on how students acquire knowledge of, and learn to interpret, the arts; how students perceive, value, perform, create, and use the arts; and how learning in the arts broadens perspective, gives a sense of the human condition, and fosters reasoning ability.

Leadership in Arts Education

The governance, education, arts and business-producer sectors should work together to convince parents and political and education leaders at the state, district, and local levels that education is complete and acceptable only when the arts are included as essential components sequentially taught. Making the case for arts education to state and local leadership is a political job requiring greater effort than it does for school subjects that large segments of the public already perceive to be basic. To this end:

A. National, state, and local arts education advocates need (i) to develop greater consensus on the objectives of arts education—what students are expected to learn at what ages, (ii) to obtain official recognition of the importance of arts education from the highest levels of political leadership — and then (iii) to work cooperatively to plan for and implement effective programs in school districts and schools (as a part of general education reform).

B. The case for arts education should be made in the same way as for any other subject: i.e., for sequential and testable instruction by qualified teachers, with high school graduation requirements that specify the arts (not in the alternative with other subjects), and with adequate time, money, curricula, and materials.

C. State education and arts agencies should work cooperatively with regional and local education and arts agencies, professional organizations, artists and arts institutions to provide leadership and support for improving arts education.

D. At the local level, community leaders (in particular the trustees of arts organizations) should work with local school boards, parent-teacher associations and schools to ensure that the arts are in fact sequentially taught in schools by qualified teachers for *all* students (not just the gifted and talented).

E. Programs should be instituted to help local school board members and education administrators understand why it is their responsibility, and thus in their interest, to make arts education a priority. These programs should help local school board members and education administrators to provide leadership for this part, as for other parts, of the curriculum.

The Role of the National Endowment for the Arts

The National Endowment for the Arts, which is to arts education what the National Science Foundation is to science education, should (i) make the case for arts education, (ii) facilitate collaboration among the four sectors concerned with arts education (governance, education, arts, business-producer) to make it a basic and sequential part of school instruction, and (iii) assist development and distribution of curricular, instructional, and assessment models for the benefit of state and local education authorities. To this end:

A. The policies and resources (staff and money) of the Endowment for arts education should be continued and strengthened over a period of at least 10 years in order to allow implementation of present policies and of the recommendations in this report to bear fruit. The Fiscal Year 1989 budget request for the Endowment's Arts in Education Program provides for such strengthening in that year.

B. The Endowment should provide the President and the Congress a report on progress in arts education in preparation for the Endowment's reauthorization in the mid-'90's (the reauthorization which follows anticipated reauthorization in 1990).

C. The Endowment should advocate the development of higher standards for state and local arts curriculum guides, courses, and curriculum materials. It should provide limited funding to assist state/local curriculum development. It should, in cooperation with the U.S. Department of Education, convene a meeting of experts to review curricular materials (including the work on curricula of the new national research centers on the arts, literature, and elementary subjects) with a view to making recommendations on arts curricula and on school programs to implement them.

D. The Endowment should work with the U.S. Department of Education to develop a plan for the inclusion of each of the arts in the National Assessment of Educational Progress. The plan should include analysis of whether arts education might best be assessed by (i) separate assessments for each of the individual arts, (ii) a general arts assessment, (iii) integrating arts assessments with other subject area assessments, or (iv) a combination of these.

E. The Endowment should provide limited funding to assist state-level development of model assessment plans, programs and procedures, both with respect to programs and student testing.

F. The Endowment should encourage (i) state education agencies and arts education associations to recruit highly qualified arts teachers; (ii) state certifying agencies to raise standards for teacher certification and teacher preparation programs accreditation; and (iii) school boards to

Frank Stella, *Quaqua! Attaccati La! 4x,* 1985, Hirshhorn Museum and Sculpture Garden, Smithsonian Institution, Washington

hire qualified arts teachers. The Endowment should encourage the arts sector to lend support to these efforts.

G. The Endowment should continue to identify areas in which there is a need for systematic and regular collection of baseline survey data on arts education, and it should disseminate the results of its studies and data to the arts education communities and the public. The Endowment should also provide limited funding to assist efforts to translate research into classroom practice.

H. The Endowment should appoint an ongoing Advisory Board (with representatives of the governance, education, arts, and business-producer sectors) whose purpose would be to institute a national dialogue on:

> (i) what students, at a minimum, should know of and about the arts when they graduate from high school, (ii) how required course units might be structured to include teaching of these minimum requirements, and (iii) what evaluation mechanisms might be appropriate and effective to assess whether students have actually mastered such materials and skills.

The Advisory Board should specifically advise the Endowment on:

> (i) activities and efforts which it could undertake to ensure that the recommendations in this report are addressed by the appropriate parties, (ii) development (with appropriate agencies and associations) of proposals for a master plan for arts assessment as part of the National Assessment of Educational Progress, (iii) development of a plan by which exemplary school and district arts programs might be identified, recognized, and rewarded (e.g., exemplary schools, programs and teachers); and (iv) the report to the President and Congress suggested for the Endowment's mid-'90's reauthorization.

I. The Endowment should provide a national model for the kind of collaboration necessary to make progress in arts education. The model should in particular include the U.S. Department of Education, the National Endowment for the Humanities, and the national associations that can influence arts education. The Endowment should assist states, localities, and the arts education community generally to develop a clearer vision of what arts education in the United States can and should be.

Arts in the Classroom

Do American elementary and secondary school students learn as much about the arts as they should? Do they get the education in the arts they deserve? What are our students doing in the arts? What do they learn from what they are doing? How do their lessons in the arts relate to other school subjects? What kinds of teachers teach the arts? Are they well prepared?

There are no ready answers to these questions. There are more than 15,000 school districts in America, 59,082 public elementary schools, 23,947 public secondary schools, and over 25,000 private schools. Each is different.

The strengths and weaknesses of arts education are not very different from the strengths and weaknesses found in the teaching—and learning — of other subjects. In the arts, as in other subjects, *more* education often does not guarantee *better* education. More instructional time and more homework do not necessarily signify more opportunities to explore ideas, develop theories, apply principles, or appreciate civilization.

Elementary classroom teachers, responsible for teaching the full array of school subjects, are generally no better trained in science than in art. In high school, it is the college-bound student who is likely to be exposed to the thought of the molders of civilization, rather than the average student or one in need of remedial work. This is as true for the arts as for the sciences and the humanities.

Perhaps the best way to convey a sense of what students actually experience in their education in the arts is through a series of vignettes.

BEFORE KINDERGARTEN

The arts surround children from birth. The air is filled with music. Pictures are everywhere — in books and magazines, on walls. Stories abound. Action and fantasy are the steady fare of television. Children imitate the arts of others, including other children, and then add their own twist.

Before a little girl crosses the street alone, she will have traveled to imaginary worlds and told others of her adventures. She will have invented stories, sung snatches of songs, copied and invented dances. She will have spent over three hours a day watching television. She will have discovered buildings and signs in the street. She will have drawn houses in crayon and built castles with blocks. She may not know what "art" is, but she will nevertheless have spent much of her first five years absorbing and being involved with art.

Some children are encouraged in their artistic activities and given materials to reinvent their worlds. They may have been taken to museums, concerts or a performance of *The Nutcracker.* Others have been propped up in front of a television set to become passive receivers of art, and probably not the best art.

Except for television, what happens to today's children is apparently not very different from what happened to their parents as children. Most of today's adults grew up in households where there was essentially no classical music or opera; they were also for the most part never taken to a museum or gallery or a live performance of dance, classical music or theater.

Figure 5. What Were the Childhood Arts Experiences of Today's Adults? (as polled in 1985)

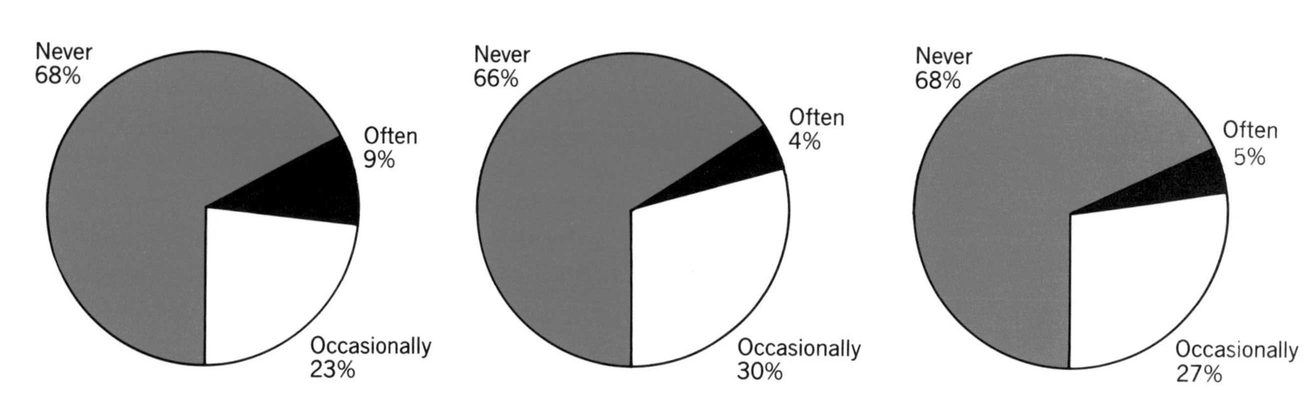

Source: Robinson, J. P., et al., "Survey of Public Participation in the Arts: for 1985, Vol. 1, Project Report," December 1986, p. 371. Prepared under Cooperative Agreement NEA CA 85-24 with the National Endowment for the Arts, Washington, D.C.

The fact is that children arrive at the schoolhouse door at different stages. For some, dancing and singing, drawing and painting, acting and telling stories, designing and building are second nature. Some have a sense of the vocabularies of the arts, just as they do of language. Others, left to the continuous ministry of television and radio, will not. Social stratifications and different kinds of families shape America's preschoolers in very different ways.

KINDERGARTEN

In the traditional kindergarten, based on Friedrich Froebel's "children's gardens" of a century-and-a-half ago, young children are educated through a structured succession of "gifts" — blocks, games, woolen balls, drawing exercises, embroidery, weaving. The purpose of the "gifts," most of which relate to the arts, is to encourage playful exploration and discovery.

Here is how it works in a traditional kindergarten in Rogerville, Tennessee. The morning begins with "free choice." There are easels for brush or finger painting, tables with scraps of paper for "cut and paste," Lego blocks to build houses and cities. There are puzzles and storybooks.

"Reading readiness" follows, with reading, telling, and making up stories. Fairy tales, *The Three Bears* and *The Little Red Hen*, teach children to be good listeners and give them a taste for children's literature. Singing the alphabet and identifying letters is a new game.

Next comes 20 minutes of music. The children sing favorite songs like "Where is Thumbkin?" or "Twinkle, Twinkle Little Star." Sometimes they listen to a classic like Prokofiev's *Peter and the Wolf.* Hearing it three or four times a year enables them to distinguish different instruments ("Tell me when you hear the drum").

Mathematics follows for about 30 minutes and includes counting, and finding and drawing shapes — three squares, four balloons, five eggs. The concepts of art pervade mathematics too. The social studies curriculum begins with "me," moves to "my family," and "my neighborhood." Children look at mirrors and draw self portraits; they draw their family, their street, the firehouse and fire engine, distilling their experience through line. The holidays — Halloween, Thanksgiving, Hanukkah and Christmas—are celebrated with both art and music.

The traditional kindergarten is, however, disappearing in the wake of parents' longing for "superbabies" — for high test scores and "achieving" children. In these new kindergartens the arts are being displaced by the word and number drills formerly taught in first grade, despite lack of evidence that this approach in kindergarten actually results in higher test scores.

Today's more "academic" kindergarten emphasizes learning the letters of the alphabet and the sounds the letters make. The children learn reading through phonics, cut out pictures of objects and animals whose names begin with the same letter, learn to print their names, and even write short sentences. They count numbers aloud, learn sequence and the concept of quantity. While the traditional kindergarten provided a bridge to symbols based on the arts, the academic kindergarten is based on learning symbols.

Some children find the academic kindergarten exciting and

satisfying; others, not yet ready to learn symbols, may be bewildered and frustrated.

ELEMENTARY SCHOOL

The problems facing today's elementary school are far more complex than even a decade ago, especially for the regular classroom teachers. In addition to the traditional courses in reading, writing, and arithmetic, they are expected to cover such diverse new areas of study as drug abuse, safety, computer skills, hygiene, and English as a second language. The U.S. Department of Education 1987 survey of a national sample of school districts (1987 district survey) estimates that 12 percent of elementary school instructional time is devoted to the arts (primarily visual art and music).

Finding time to teach the arts and other subjects sequentially and knowledgeably in the face of all these other demands is not easy. Resources are scarce. The 1987 district survey shows that many school districts are operating without the benefit of district-recommended or required texts in the arts. Further, while only 16 percent of elementary schools lack music specialists, 42 percent lack visual arts specialists.

Figure 6. Percent of Instructional Time 1986-87 Allotted to the Arts and Other Subjects, Grades 1-8

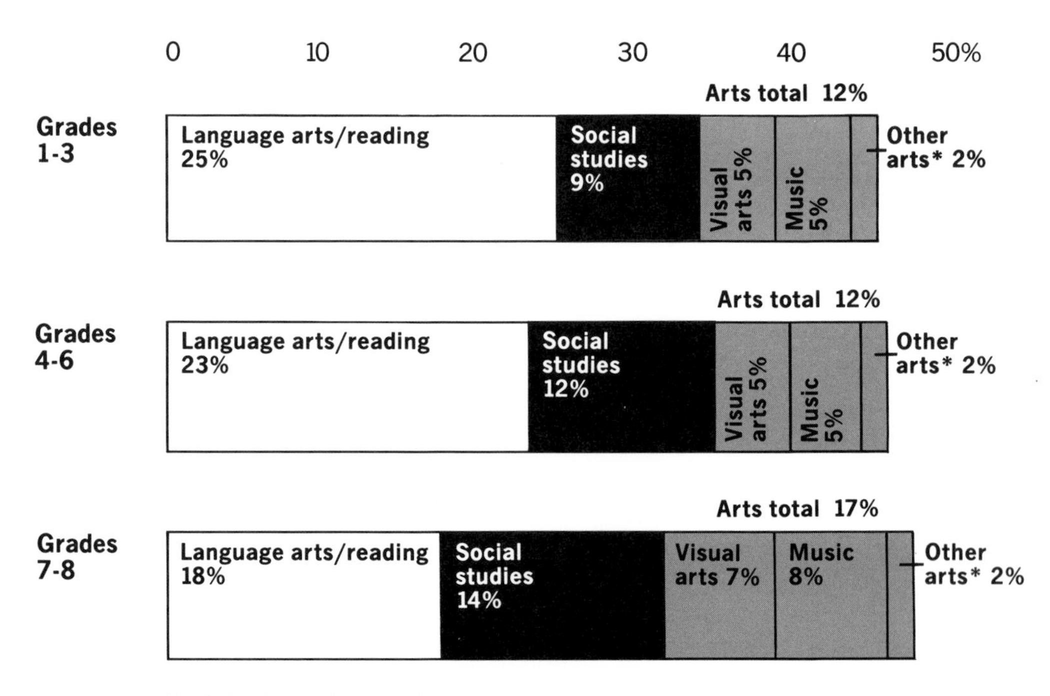

*Includes dance, drama and creative writing.

Source: Center for Education Statistics, "Public School District Policies and Practices in Selected Aspects of Arts and Humanities Instruction," U.S. Department of Education Bulletin, February 1988, Figure 3, p. 7.

There are also regional differences: in the West over one-fifth of the schools lack music specialists, and over one-half lack visual arts specialists. (See Figure 2, p. 23.) And, even when schools have specialist teachers, one specialist may have as many as 600 students a week in three separate schools, and be required to relate arts projects to the specific curriculums of each of 28 classroom teachers.

And yet, if a child is to develop a lifelong appreciation of the arts, the early years are critical.

Visual Art in Second Grade With a Special Teacher

While many smaller towns have no art specialists, the children of Pine Grove Mills, in rural central Pennsylvania, know that one of the most special times of the week is when the teacher says: "Let me know when it's 10:30 and time to go to art."

These second graders see the art teacher once a week for 40 minutes. The class is one of 28 this hard-pressed and conscientious teacher has; she attempts to relate her art projects to the curriculum of each of these classes. This teacher teaches 600 students in three separate schools in a single week.

Today, the second graders are going to make "dinosaurs." The teacher shows them how a ball of clay can be shaped into a dinosaur, and then the children make their own, just like the ones they studied in science. The room is nearly silent, activity intense, and clean-up at the end of the class elicits a chorus of groans. But another class is waiting at the door. During the 30 additional times the children come to art class during the year, they will design a game; make toys; make compositions of colors, lines, and shapes; and paint a mural of Holland. They will do projects to accompany the holidays, make collages, learn the difference between warm and cool colors, make prints with stencils, do appliqué work and make puppets and stuffed "furry things."

The art teacher shows them pictures she brings with her of ships, trains, planes, cowboys, and castles. There are posters and children's art, but few, if any, original works of art. Since the instruction is mainly aimed at crafts, popular art and illustration, the students learn little or nothing about the great masterworks, except when the teacher presents on sailcloth color reproductions that she takes from school to school.

An Elementary School Filled With Music

At Eisenhower Elementary School in Norman, Oklahoma, school begins with "Good Morning Eisenhower," an assembly which opens to the strains of Aaron Copland's "Fanfare for the Common Man." In "Good Morning Eisenhower," after reciting the Pledge of Allegiance, the children sing folk songs and patriotic songs, hear announcements, and perhaps watch their fellow students perform a short play they have written and rehearsed. The "Good Morning Eisenhower" assembly is a 14-year tradition which takes place every day except Wednesdays, and teachers and parents are always invited to attend.

On Wednesdays, the children stay in their classrooms to listen to "The Eisenhower School Radio Show." They may listen to an excerpt from Dvořák's *New World* Symphony and be asked for their responses to it. Or, they may hear a recorded version of a Hans Christian Andersen story, or listen to poetry, a story, or a schoolmate's play.

At Eisenhower School, the roll is often sung so that each child can get to know his or her own voice. The teacher sings, "Mat-thew Rogers," and Matt sings back, "Mat-thew Rogers." Children who come into the classroom are often frightened by the prospect of singing, but soon they too are comfortably echoing the voice of the teacher.

In the fourth grade, all students learn to play the recorder, taught by a music specialist. This continues in the fifth grade, and interested students may enroll in a stringed instrument class, which includes 22 children. One student brings his bass to class to show the others how big it is, how it is held and the ways it can be played. Each child is given an opportunity to draw the bow or pluck the strings. They will also listen to Benjamin Britten's "The Young Person's Guide to the Orchestra," and discuss the families of instruments and the sounds they make.

At Eisenhower, music is not simply relegated to the music room. A committee of teachers assists the music teacher with the morning assembly and the Wednesday radio programs. The principal notes that Eisenhower students score, on the average, at or above grade-level in all tested subjects. "What makes us different from other schools is how we use all the subjects — especially the arts — to help our children learn self-discipline, connect one part of their learning with another, and use divergent and creative thinking as part of their decision-making process. In the arts, there is problem solving going on that can't be done when kids just fill out workbook pages."

Art Goes to School in New Jersey

A fourth-grade classroom in Delaware Valley, New Jersey, displays color reproductions of Brueghel's frenzied *Wedding Dance*, Mondrian's modern grids and primary colors, a Rembrandt and a Chagall. The children are asked: "What kinds of lines are in the picture?" "What colors has the artist used?" "How do they make you feel?"

The class is guided by a parent, one of a volunteer group of approximately 700 who conduct art appreciation programs for 125,000 children in 10 counties once a year. These children attend schools which find it difficult to teach art appreciation because many art and classroom teachers are not prepared to do this. In this case, as in many others, the gap is partially filled by concerned parents and volunteers, to whom arts education in the United States owes an enormous debt. But they cannot solve the overall problem; nor should they.

As one of the volunteers in this program says, "At this point we are offering what the arts teachers are not doing. We do things that art teachers are not prepared to do. We give our volunteers intensive workshops about artists, history, technique, and style."

Elementary Schools Without Arts Specialists

In a high mountain valley in Preston, Idaho, the half-dozen small community grade schools that flourished 50 years ago have been consolidated into one enormous year-round school for 1,200 students. None of its teachers is specially trained in the visual, literary, performing or media arts.

The writing portion of the state-designated fourth-grade language arts program (600 minutes a week) is determined by textbook. The teacher follows a 36-lesson plan that emphasizes "pre-writing," editing, and the final draft. Based on models, the students read a folktale before writing one. However, the teacher goes beyond the lesson plan to have her students write poetry four or five times a year. They learn about couplets, meter and stanzas, and they write haiku. The reading textbook includes excerpts from writers such as Laura Ingalls Wilder and E. B. White, with the suggestion that the originals be read in their entirety. But the complete books are not available in the school library, although they are on the acquisition list.

This fourth-grade teacher has strengths in writing and music, but not in the visual arts. "I teach mainly crafts," she says. "We do things for Christmas and the other holidays, make Indian villages, totem heads, vegetable prints, blow ink across the paper with straws, and make Indian sand painting on sandpaper. The children don't seem to mind if we skip art for a week." There is no focus on works of art in the Idaho curriculum.

Music is taught once a week for 35 to 40 minutes and consists mainly of singing. Seven fourth-grade classes are brought together for music. Although each of the seven classroom teachers helps, only three have sufficient background in music to play the piano or lead the singing. As one of them says, "We are trying to make it more than 36 songs, and we have recently started to learn about meter, rhythm, and composers, but the [teachers] who don't know music just have the children listen to some cute song."

There is no dance program in the fourth grade, and drama is a once-a-year affair when *The Reluctant Dragon*, Bill Cosby's *Tonsils* or *Paddington Turns Detective* is done with narrators instead of actors speaking the lines.

This Idaho approach is not uncommon. When the language arts

textbook presents a comprehensive sequential program, or when the teacher has special strengths, creative writing will be taught seriously. Otherwise, it will not. Dance or drama is seldom taught and children are not encouraged to use their visual imagination. The media and design arts are generally ignored, and there is little or no attempt to introduce children to great works of art, past or present.

Learning About Architecture and Design

More than any other art forms, architecture and design determine the quality of our lives. The products of these artistic disciplines are ultimately purchased by every citizen in America. Among these products are the houses in which we live, the automobiles we drive, and the landscape, neighborhoods, towns and cities which are so much a part of the lives of all Americans. Yet, almost nothing related to these artistic disciplines is taught in schools. There are few curricula on design, and teachers are generally not educated to teach it. Currently, in most cases, the only way in which these disciplines are taught, if at all, is where practicing architects and designers themselves go into the schools.

In Philadelphia, Pennsylvania, in an older neighborhood of small row houses and narrow streets, a third-year professional architect, whose firm encouraged him to do so, visited a fifth-grade class once a week for eight weeks. The school was of pre-World War I vintage. More than 80 percent of the students were Black; others were children of recent immigrants from places like Korea and Vietnam.

The architect showed them slides — tents and tent forms, round thatched-roof African mud houses, European churches and palaces, the Colosseum in Rome, and Le Corbusier's modern chapel at Ronchamp. Although few students had traveled beyond their own neighborhoods, they were engaged by the slides and did not hesitate to make guesses about the location and function of these unfamiliar buildings. They also looked at their own neighborhood, analyzed the materials and drew the floor plans and facades of their homes. They related the architectural styles of their streets to those in other parts of the world. As a final project, they designed and built a model of a new theater for their neighborhood, a cylinder 36 inches in diameter and 30 inches high. They exhibited the model to the rest of the school to the accompaniment of a "pretend" concert by the rock group "The New Edition."

By the end of these eight weeks, the students could look at their neighborhood with new eyes. They had also begun to develop ideas about their dream house and dream community. While this short-term experience was meaningful to these students, the imperative for public education is to develop an educational process whereby this fleeting

Opposite: Amiens Cathedral, courtesy of the French Government Tourist Office, New York

residency experience might be built on with ongoing and sequential instruction.

Drama in a Texas Fifth-Grade Classroom

If drama is taught in elementary grades, it is generally a part of English studies. Few teachers are required to take special courses in drama, and only 13 of the 50 states enable an elementary teacher to be specially certified in drama (see Figure 16, pp. 106-107).

An exception can be found in a fifth-grade classroom in Austin, Texas, a state with a tradition of teaching drama in the schools. Here drama is taught by a teacher who studied it at university. The students do sensory pantomime, acting out the flavors of their favorite foods. They dramatize folktales such as "Stone Soup," myths like "Pandora," and stories like "The Three Billy Goats Gruff," "Little Red Riding Hood," "Rapunzel," and "Cinderella."

Television-age children are often not familiar with these stories, but in this classroom the classics of children's literature become, through the act of re-creation, the special possessions of fifth-graders. By acting them out, the children come to understand what motivates the characters, understand the plot structure, and learn how settings, props, lights, and costumes combine to create dramatic spectacle. They learn to appreciate the literary sources of drama and to make aesthetic judgments about it. They also learn how to work together.

MIDDLE AND JUNIOR HIGH SCHOOL

The 1987 district survey estimates that 17 percent of instructional time in grades seven and eight is devoted to the arts, primarily visual arts and music (see Figure 6, p. 50). For many students, the last time they will be required to study the arts is in middle school, or junior high school. Middle schools usually include grades six, seven, and eight; sometimes five, six, seven, and eight. Junior high schools include grades seven through nine. These are the years when adolescents develop an overwhelming interest in the popular culture. Middle and junior high schools thus have the challenge of engaging students in the universe of art that lies outside the popular culture of the moment, in the face of heavy marketing by the entertainment industry and peer pressure from the high school idols whom middle and junior high schoolers emulate.

General Music

The 1987 district survey reports that less than half the nation's seventh and eighth grade students are enrolled in "general music," although in the Northeast the proportion is 81 percent and in the West only 21 percent. (See Figure 3, p. 24.) The "general music" course might be offered for one nine-week period, once a week for a year, or every day for a semester. In some states, even students who take band or chorus are required to take general music, while in other states they are exempt.

Some teachers complain that students don't like general music, and that these classes "are full of discipline problems." True, in some general music classes, students are required to sit and listen to what strikes them as an interminable series of recorded selections and to learn by rote the names of notes or elements of music or music theory. But this need not be so.

In a seventh-grade general music course in Bucyrus, Ohio, the students sing or do rhythm activities in every class so as to grasp a musical concept and deepen their appreciation. Each class involves performance, study, analysis, and examination of the relationship between the popular music the students know and the music the teacher wants them to understand.

For example, they will listen to, sing, and study the traditional Shaker song, "Simple Gifts," and compare it to Aaron Copland's "Appalachian Spring," in which the composer incorporates variations on the "Simple Gifts" theme. They will discuss why and how he borrowed the tune, whether this is "cheating," and how it helps to express the feeling of an Appalachian spring.

They will study Copland's career, noting that although he studied in France, it was America and American music that he celebrated in his own music. The students also listen to ways television commercials sometimes incorporate themes from well-known compositions, and discuss how Carly Simon used "Eensy-Weensy Spider" in the movie *Heartburn*. Finally, the students will make and perform their own variations on the simple themes they have heard.

Visual Art

In a typical junior high school, seventh graders for the first time have to deal with different teachers for different subjects. They also meet a visual arts teacher who majored in art at college and now has a certificate to teach it. In a typical class, the students work in a special art room with high ceilings and bright light. The walls are covered from floor to ceiling with tack board for the display of the students' art. Three times a week for the next half year, students can carve reliefs, model in clay, paint in watercolor, make ceramic pots, design enameled jewelry, and make prints from linoleum blocks.

Because both the state curriculum guide and the curriculum prepared by the art teachers call for study of design, the teacher will integrate design concepts and techniques into nearly every lesson. The district curriculum also has a section on "knowing about and understanding art, artists and cultures." Four of the 54 art periods will be devoted to studying such Impressionist and Post-Impressionist painters as Monet, Renoir, Seurat, Gauguin, and Van Gogh. However, the curriculum guide, which carefully outlines a grade-by-grade developmental sequence for each major area of art-making, does not list works of art which students should recognize; nor does it prescribe a grade-by-grade sequence for the study of the history of art.

In short, art is taught almost solely as "making art," as it has been since these students entered kindergarten. In the teacher's view, the purpose of teaching art is "to enhance students' awareness of the world around them." She is more concerned with this than with exposing her class to the themes of great art, past and present.

HIGH SCHOOL

Educational reform has had its most dramatic effect on high schools. State-mandated graduation requirements now include more coursework generally and more designated specific courses. In some states, the length of the high school year, as well as the high school day, has been extended. An increasing number of states now list a unit of the arts as a part of graduation requirements, and many high schools offer a variety of arts courses as electives, mostly oriented toward creation and performance. However, as Figure 7 indicates, except for English, which is required for high school graduation everywhere, enrollment in arts courses is low.

Therefore, while high school reforms which place greater emphasis on the arts are clearly steps in the right direction, they do not automatically ensure that students graduate with more knowledge, understanding or appreciation of the arts.

Music

About one in three students enrolls in some kind of music course during high school—band, orchestra, choir, or music appreciation. The typical high school music program revolves around performances: a fall parents' open house concert, Christmas and Hanukkah concerts, spring concerts, and possibly a musical production. A graduation concert rounds out the year.

Preparation for the first performance can start on the first day of school. The teachers want their groups to sound good, so they select the music in terms of what is realistic to expect them to play well. While the complexity and subtlety of the music increases during the year and the quality of musicianship may improve, little attention is given to designing a program that is stylistically or thematically connected.

Most high school music teachers were performers themselves, and this sets the tone for most high school music programs. Even if the football team isn't winning, the band will at least sound and look good; this matters to those parents and students who have invested time and money since elementary school in learning how to play an instrument. The performance bias is also evident in the amounts of money schools

Figure 7. High School Course Offerings and Enrollments, 1981-82 (50 States and D.C.)

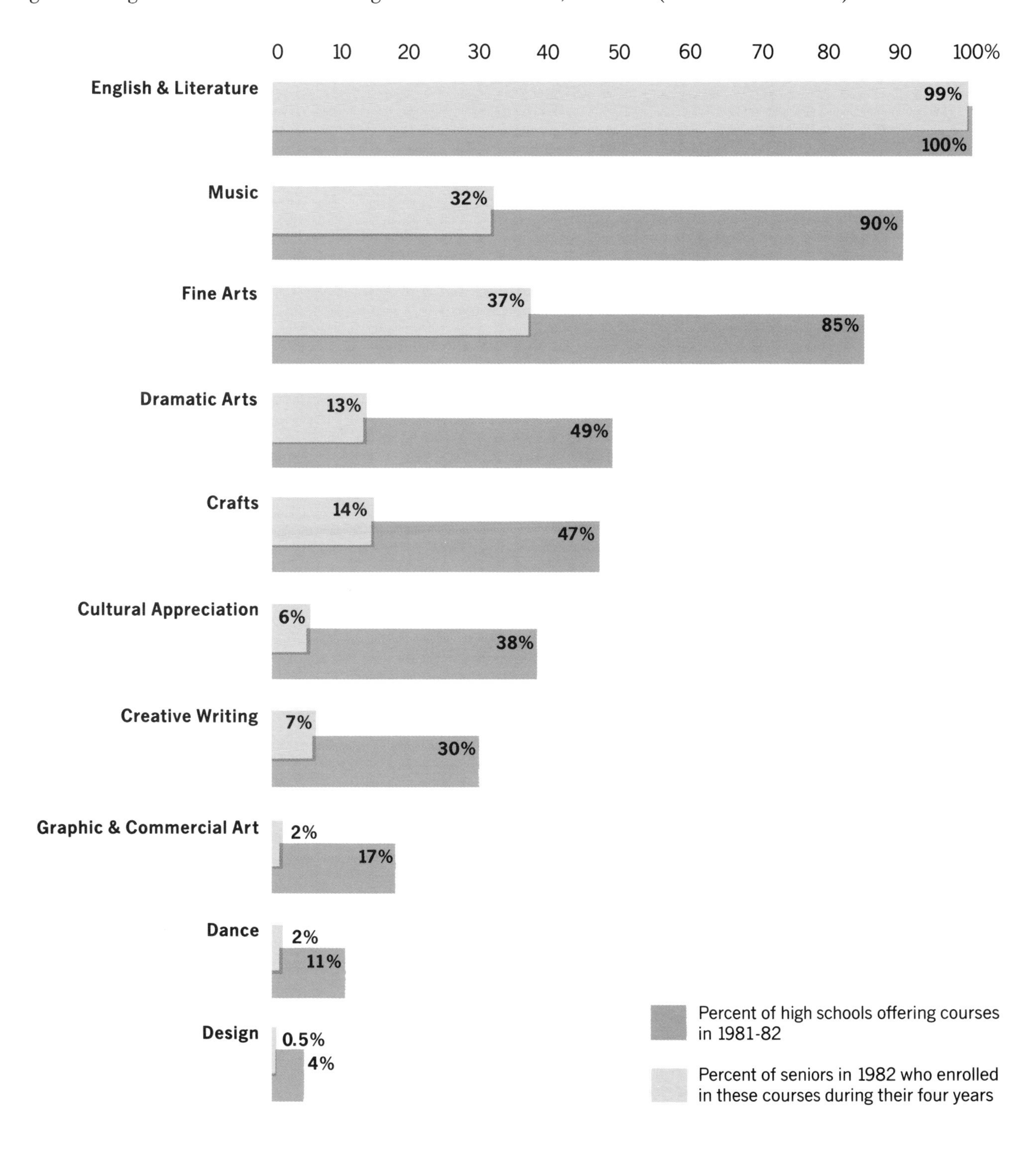

Source: Evaluation Technologies, Inc. "Course Offerings and Enrollments in the Arts and the Humanities at the Secondary School Level," National Center for Education Statistics, U.S. Department of Education, Washington, D.C., 1984, Table 1, p. 18.

invest in band uniforms and choral robes compared to what they spend on recordings or books.

Theory, composition, and music history may seem of little importance to students intent on mastering the trumpet part of four Sousa marches. But without it, these students will know nothing of the great variety of music and the place of Sousa marches in music history; the great heritage of music will be denied them.

There are always exceptions, and some high schools do offer courses in music appreciation. But the performance bias, central to most high school music programs, contributes to the perception that arts education is, or should be, entertainment rather than serious learning. It also contributes to the assumption that the arts may require certain skills, but there is nothing about them that requires real learning.

School Bands

Band recruiting typically begins in the fifth or sixth grade. While some districts go to great lengths to identify and test talented children, in others the music teacher simply asks for volunteers. In a typical junior high school, band may be taken as a course by anywhere from 30 to 150 students. Seventh, eighth, and ninth graders rehearse together, the experienced students carrying the inexperienced. While there is little individual instruction in school, many students take private lessons, often from the band director.

The results of all this are clearly seen in high school. On crisp Friday evenings in October in communities across the country, the high-stepping bands that play rollicking tunes at half-time bring feelings of local pride. Some bands compete in area, state, regional, or national competitions where technical skills and long rehearsals pay off. Ironically, the band that ranks educationally at the lower end of the educational spectrum, concentrating on three or four well-rehearsed pieces, is the one that may appear to the public, at least, to be the most successful. It will win competitions, and once the trophy has been won, will immediately begin rehearsal on the three or four pieces for next year. The technical skill of the young performers may be exceptional, but their understanding of the music they perform may be seriously lacking.

Even so, if the school maintains a balance among the educational, entertainment and competitive aspects of marching bands, the band can be a vital factor in music education. It is fair to say that high school bands have probably done more than any other single institution to make live music a part of American life.

Visual Art

Most students enroll in high school art classes voluntarily, if they enroll at all. They may be interested in a particular medium—paint, ceramics, stained glass, or printmaking; or they may want to learn how art and design can lead to a commercial career. Whatever their motivation, they generally find the art studio a friendly and efficient place where they are free to advance their own individual interests and where materials and equipment are easily available.

Education in the visual arts, however, attracts far less public notice than performing arts education. The band is likely to be supported by a parents' booster club, and music students as a matter of course gain recognition through their performances. On the other hand, high school visual arts students have few opportunities to exhibit their work and to achieve recognition for it.

English Classes and the Arts: Literature

The one art form to which nearly all high school students are introduced is literature. Novels, short stories, poems, and drama are universally taught as types of writing. But comprehensive study of the best of literature in the English language is usually reserved only for the college-bound.

Students in honors or advanced placement classes might study three or more Shakespearean plays such as *Hamlet, Macbeth,* and *Julius Caesar.* Those not on a college track will probably read only one, generally *Romeo and Juliet.* College-bound students are also more likely to read entire books rather than excerpts. Thus the great works of language are denied to that half of the student population who will not go on to college. They deserve better.

Even the best literature programs do little to help students understand how major themes have been dealt with through the ages within different cultural perspectives and among various art forms. Rare is the high school where its students study and probe the star-crossed tragedy of *Romeo and Juliet* in its many artistic forms: Shakespeare's play, Prokofiev's ballet, Gounod's opera, Franco Zeffirelli's film, and Leonard Bernstein's *West Side Story.* Such a multifaceted approach would show students some of the many ways in which great artists portray the human condition.

Creative Writing

Although about 30 percent of public high schools offer courses in creative writing, fewer than 7 percent of students enroll in them. The quality of instruction offered may have something to do with this. For while teachers of music, theater, dance, and the visual arts usually practice their art while they teach, this is not the case with teachers of creative writing. Usually trained as English teachers, they have acquired skills in grammar analysis and in literary history and criticism rather than in creative writing. Many excellent in-service training courses in the teaching of writing are now being offered around the country to improve instruction in the craft of writing, both within the regular English curriculum and in specialized courses.

The School Literary Magazine

Young poets and story writers need to be published, and the school literary magazine is likely to be the first step. The magazine may be directed by a teacher or an editorial board. It might be photocopied—or carefully designed, extensively illustrated, typeset, and printed on fine quality paper. The Columbia Scholastic Press Association estimates that about one-third of the nation's high schools publish some type of literary magazine.

In some high schools, literary magazines become the fiefdom of a small group of students and a faculty advisor who use it to further their own aspirations. But at Flagstaff High School in northern Arizona, with a school population of "Anglos," Navajo and Hopi native Americans, Black and Chicano students, the advisor attempts to publish writing by a cross-section of students. Some of these students thought they couldn't get their work published. But the teacher encouraged them, pointing out that Jack London hadn't been interested in school. One student dropped out of school before his poem was published, but after he came back and when his poem was mentioned by the Columbia Scholastic Press Association, he ordered five copies of the magazine. In 1986, the magazine was awarded a medal by the association and was rated excellent by the National Council of Teachers of English.

SPECIAL PROBLEMS

Dance: New Recognition for an Old Art Form

As the President of the National Dance Association remarked when asked to characterize it, dance in American schools is "virtually non-existent, just little pockets here and there." In 1985, no state required elementary school classroom teachers to take a course in dance, and only 15 made provision for secondary school teachers to be certified to teach dance.

While elementary school students might practice and perform folk and square dances for a yearly performance, and middle, junior, and senior high schools might have two, four, or six-week units of dance as a part of physical education, dance is rarely treated seriously as an art. Few physical education instructors are prepared to teach dance, and dance, exercise, and sports do not always coexist congenially in the curriculum.

At the request of the National Dance Association, Margaret Pappalardo and her associates surveyed dance education in Massachusetts in 1987, and learned that a Massachusetts student had less than a one-in-five chance of attending a school with a dance program.

Suburban schools were twice as likely to have such programs as urban or rural schools, but only a third of the schools offering dance had a trained teacher, and only about 40 percent of them offered a year-long course. In three-quarters of the schools, dance was a branch of physical education; and one-third of the schools considered aerobic exercise to be dance, although most specialists did not.

Dance education is probably much the same outside of Massachusetts. Only about 10 states have generated thoughtful curriculum guides in dance, and these have been developed only since 1982, according to the executive director of the National Dance Association.

Media Arts: Film, Television, and Radio

Because it takes a very long time for a new art form to become established as a basic part of the school curriculum, courses in film, television, and radio are relatively rare in American schools. A notable exception is the high school in Apple Valley, Minnesota, which has a comprehensive arts program in which the media arts play an important part. During the winter trimester, four different instructors teach 10 different sections of a film course offered by the Communications Department along with English, literature, and speech. Apple Valley High considers film an essential component of communications.

The film course includes the history of film and of different film genres — historical films, Westerns, mysteries, science fiction, etc. Students learn how to evaluate film themes, plots, scripts, acting, setting, costumes and makeup, sound, photography, direction, and editing. Assisted by a text (Johnson and Bone, 1986) and by a video tape on film criticism prepared by the course instructors, they read examples of film criticism, watch television film critics, and try their hand at writing criticism. Most important, they analyze the influence of film on American society: for example, the impact of the movie, *Bonnie and Clyde,* in which vicious outlaws become cult heroes to a generation.

But even in Apple Valley, the new medium of television is not yet studied. And so, encouragingly, the Apple Valley Communications Department is planning a new course, "Mass Media," in which students will analyze the relationships between hard news and entertainment, visual and oral presentations, TV programs and commercials, and consider such issues as how minority groups are presented on television. Students completing these courses will have reached a level of critical insight into the most pervasive media of our time that is available to pitifully few American high school students.

SPECIAL RESOURCES FOR THE ARTS

In many schools, student experience with the arts is more profound than the foregoing examples might indicate. There are schools with artist residency programs that bring students and teachers together with professional artists. There are school districts that foster the arts in magnet high schools specializing in the arts. A few high schools offer special classes to students taking the Advanced Placement Examination in music or visual arts.

Artists and Students Together

The Great Valley School District in Devault, Pennsylvania, has recently revised its high school arts program to include dance, theater, music, and the visual arts. As a result, one Great Valley high school student had the opportunity to work with a gifted drama teacher/director while playing the challenging role of the deaf girl in *Children of a Lesser God*. As part of the program, she and the rest of the cast spent four days in workshops with Mark Medoff, guest director and author of the play.

Great Valley students interested in dance have seen performances by the Joffrey II dancers, the Washington Ballet, and the North Carolina Dance Theatre. Others have attended performances by the Annapolis Brass Quintet, the Minikin Opera, and The Acting Company. Those interested in the visual arts can take a sequential course on great masters of painting and sculpture.

Playwright Mark Medoff writes: "At Great Valley High School, an assistant superintendent, like a Pied Piper, woos a superintendent, a principal and an entire school board—not just to follow but walk side by side with him—and thus to make the arts *acceptable* again for students who may *still* end up as engineers and computer scientists and MBAs."

A Magnet High School for the Arts

Special magnet schools have proliferated during the last decade. According to a 1984-85 survey by the National Art Education Association, at least 37 states have them. The oldest is the High School of Music and Art in New York City which opened its doors in 1938 (and in 1961 joined the High School for the Performing Arts, founded in the 1940's). But more recently, magnet schools have been established to help large, city school systems achieve greater racial balance among schools.

Nonetheless, high schools of the arts are now becoming recognized for their own sake, as well as for their role in the community. Magnet high schools open their doors both to general students interested in the arts and to those — often less than half of the student body — who seek careers in the arts.

One high school for the arts in Milwaukee, Wisconsin, in a run-down neighborhood close to museums and performing arts centers, was turned into a magnet school so as to bring a sense of mission to an institution that had fallen on hard times. With a little paint, some murals, and the conversion of a gym to a dance studio and an industrial arts room and cafeteria to an art studio and gallery, the school, originally built for 1,800 students, now enrolls 680, all of them interested or talented in the arts.

Although this Milwaukee high school employs teachers in all areas, arts teachers are preponderant. Additionally, each instructor of a non-art subject, as well as administrators and counselors, has taken at least 12 semester hours of college credit in the arts. While the state-mandated general curriculum is followed, the arts are made central, and science and social studies teachers organize their courses around the arts. Works of art are made focal points for the study of history, and relationships are drawn between works of art and literature, creative writing, and dance. Although each of the city's high schools offers visual arts, music, creative writing and theater, dance is found only in this magnet school.

The problem with such high schools for the arts is that they may reinforce the belief that the arts are only for the specially talented. Alternatively, by attracting interested and talented students and teachers, they encourage the impression that the arts are alive and well in all the schools, when in reality this is true for only a few. It is also possible that arts high schools are siphoning off gifted students and teachers who could enrich other schools, a particular problem if the base student population is small. In addition, the presence of magnet schools can serve as an alibi for other schools not to commit themselves and their resources to basic sequential arts instruction for everyone.

Art History in High School: The Advanced Placement Program

Almost every high school in the country offers courses in visual arts production and in music performance. But less than 40 percent of them offer courses in "cultural appreciation" (e.g., in history of music, dance, film or drama; in criticism, or in the arts of many cultures). And fewer than 7 percent of high school students actually take these courses. These findings parallel those of the Arts Endowment's Survey of Public Participation in the Arts of adult Americans. (See Figure 4, p. 34.)

Yet, in those few places where art history is taught seriously, many benefits occur. In a lower-middle-class area of Virginia Beach, Virginia, only seven students register for the year-long senior-year Advanced Placement Art History course, but the principal allows the class to continue, believing that art history is critical to understanding civilization and in sharpening the students' ability to analyze and master other subjects. The principal also notes that the small number of high school students taking the course is not disproportionate to the small number of students taking the examination nationally.

The text for the course is the book that is widely used in introductory college courses, Janson's *History of Art*. But the students use the book in ways seldom required of college students. Before the year is out, they will have written a 75-word analysis of each of the nearly 1,000 works of art illustrated in the text. Two or three times a week, they will write timed essays of five or 10 minutes. One day they are shown two slides: one of Venus de Milo and the other of an abstract female form by the modern sculptor, Arp. They are asked to analyze the characteristics of each and then make inferences about the conditions in the two societies that might have influenced the forms of these two sculptors. Most essays follow the form of the questions on the Advanced Placement Examination they will take at the end of the year.

The students are so well prepared when they complete this course that they score well above average for advanced placement status at college.

CONCLUSIONS

This series of vignettes is intended to illustrate something of what actually goes on in our nation's classrooms and to put flesh on the bones of the national data sources.

In general arts education in America is characterized by *imbalance*, *inconsistency*, and *inaccessibility*. There is a curricular *imbalance* in the relationship between the study of art and the performance and creation of art. There is *inconsistency* in the arts education students receive in various parts of the country, in different school districts within states, in different schools within school systems, and even in classrooms within schools. Because of the pressures on the school day, a comprehensive and sequential arts education is *inaccessible* except to a very few and often only to those with talent or a special interest.

In Elementary School

The arts receive only a modest allocation of time in elementary classrooms. The average in grades one through six is 5 percent of instructional time (74-79 minutes per week) for visual arts and 5 percent (76-84 minutes per week) for music, with only 2 percent allotted to *all* the other arts. These allocations fall short of the minimum standards of the National Art Education Association (which calls for a minimum of 100 minutes per week for visual arts) and of the Music Educators National Conference (which calls for 100 minutes per week or 7 percent of instruction time, whichever is greater, for music).

- The lack of arts specialists in many schools raises questions about the quality and effectiveness of what little time is given to the arts. The 1987 district survey indicates that over 40 percent of elementary schools lack access to visual arts specialists (almost 60 percent in the western region). Music specialists are more generally available (only 12 percent of the nation's schools are without them), but they are distributed unevenly among regions. Elementary school specialists in the other arts are essentially nonexistent.

- Elementary school classroom teachers receive little support to assist their work in arts education. Frequently, they work without the benefit of a district arts coordinator or supervisor, and have little access to books and other resource materials to enable them to present well-coordinated comprehensive arts instruction. Only 37 percent of the districts in our survey had available a list of recommended or required textbooks in the visual arts; in music, only slightly more than half the districts had such a list.

- Elementary school arts instruction focuses on popular crafts, dance, and music rather than on fostering understanding of the major works of lasting importance to civilization. Although the instruction provides opportunities for students to create and perform in some of the arts, our elementary schools do not generally provide students with even rudimentary information about important works of art.

In Junior High and Middle School

In grades seven and eight, the average time spent on the arts increases as compared to the elementary years, with an estimated 17 percent of instructional time dedicated to the arts, versus 12 percent in the elementary years.

- The same characteristics, however — imbalance, inconsistency, and inaccessibility—mark arts education at the junior high level. Fewer than half of seventh and eighth grade students take general music (48 percent), and slightly more than half (53 percent) are enrolled in visual arts courses. Enrollments are lower in other art forms such as drama and dance (14 percent). There are enormous regional variations: in the Northeast, general music enrollments average 81 percent as opposed to 21 percent in the West. Junior high students are more likely to be enrolled in music in rural areas than they are in the suburbs.

In High School

The concept of general education in the arts for all students at the high school level is virtually nonexistent. Most high school arts courses are oriented toward performance and creation. The high school schedule is organized in such a way that students who wish to attend a college or university must frequently register for a number of year-long courses that leave no time for the arts.

- Data collected in the 1982-83 school year indicate that most high schools offer several courses in the arts. But the 1987 district survey indicates that only about one-third of school districts specifically require a course in the arts in order to graduate.

- Colleges and universities often do not count high school arts courses as fulfilling academic requirements, nor do they compute high school grades in the arts when determining grade-point averages. When both college entrance and high school graduation requirements do not include the arts, there is little encouragement for students to take arts courses.

- The availability of arts courses varies with the type and location of schools. Few high schools in rural areas are able to offer a broad course selection, and the rate of rural student enrollments in such courses is lower than the national average.

Pablo Picasso, *Guernica*, Museo del Prado, Madrid

Toward an Arts Curriculum

Until we know what we want teachers to teach and students to learn, we cannot articulate the skills our teachers should have, call for the resources to support instruction, and set standards for its evaluation. Without a clear understanding of what arts education should be, we cannot hold boards of education accountable for policy and support, administrators accountable for program implementation, teachers accountable for instruction, and students accountable for learning.

What belongs in the currriculum? Should it comprise all of the arts? What aspects of each discipline should be covered — production, performance, history, critical analysis? What minimal achievement should be expected — in knowledge, understanding, skills, concepts, behaviors and attitudes? What should every future citizen know of the arts in order to be culturally literate? What graduation and college entrance requirements should be mandated? What courses should be required; which should be optional? What areas of arts study might be integrated with other subjects — in the humanities or sciences? At what ages should different aspects of the arts be taught?

There is little agreement on these issues or on what constitutes a comprehensive, basic, sequentially structured arts education program for K-12 students. While practically every state and many school districts have curriculum guides in the arts, they are often not followed. In any case, the guides seldom outline an appropriate sequence of instruction or draw on the most respected theoretical thinking in the field.

Developing an adequate arts curriculum is a challenging task. The scope and breadth of the subject matter is enormous. There is a growing consensus that arts curricula should include study of the great works of art from all times and cultures, those that probe the nature of man and reveal us to ourselves. Such works are timeless. *Oedipus Rex* is as powerful as it was when Sophocles wrote it. Beethoven's "Ode to Joy" continues to inspire us. Picasso's *Guernica,* through a series of images, reminds us of man's brutality and the horrors of war.

Arts education need not be confined to arts courses per se. History and foreign languages, for example, can have a deeper meaning for students when the arts are part of them. Such integration can begin even in elementary years. It would not necessarily require more class time — it might require less class time — but it would require changes in textbooks and selected readings and additional teamwork among teachers.

Arts curricula and lesson plans — whether for arts courses per se or for courses where the arts are integrated — must not only be taught

Figure 8. Percentage of Districts Having Arts Requirements for High School Graduation in 1981-82 and 1986-87 (50 States and D.C.)

In certain instances, local school districts may set more stringent or specific graduation requirements than state government. Some states do not generate high school graduation requirements in any subject. This chart complements Figure 1.

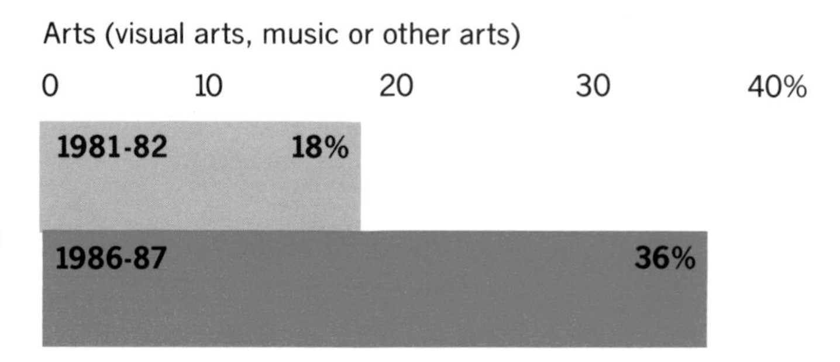

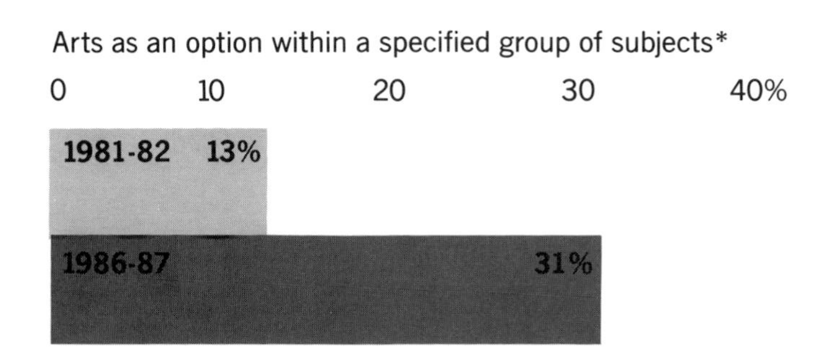

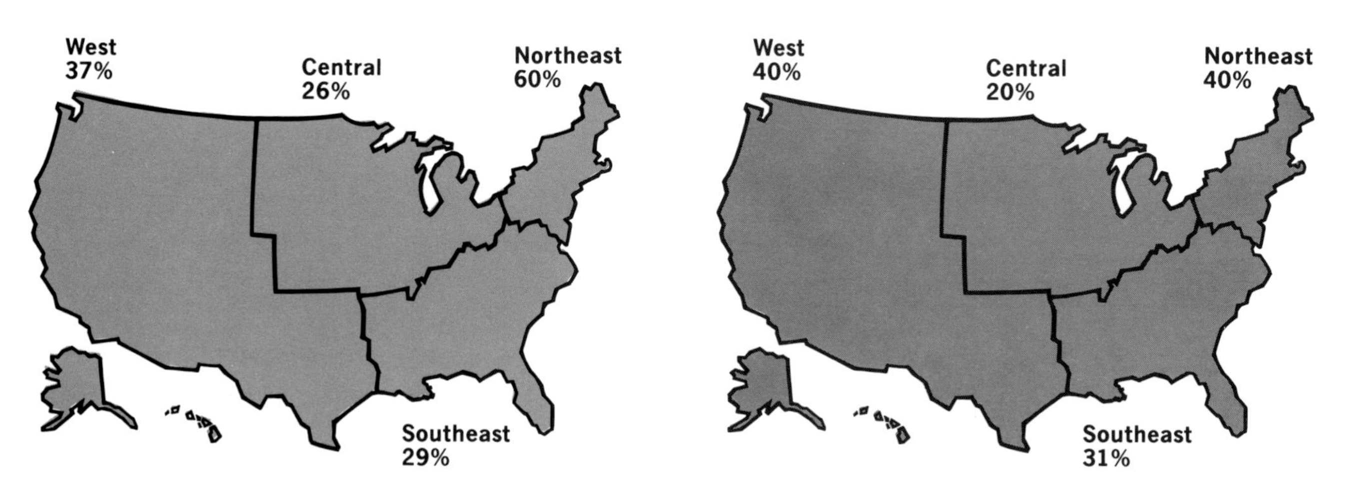

*Arts as an option refers to a requirement in which arts courses are one of several possible credit options used to fulfill a type of credit requirement (e.g., arts or foreign language or computer science).

Source: Center for Education Statistics, "Public School District Policies and Practices in Selected Aspects of Arts and Humanities Instruction," U.S. Department of Education Bulletin, February 1988, Figure 1, p. 5 and Table 5, p. 19.

but be designed. Time must be provided for teachers to prepare and for students to learn. Schedules must be arranged so that teachers can teach focused, sequential lessons that include study of masterworks. Learning must build on foundations built in prior grades.

Secretary of Education William J. Bennett proposed in December 1987 a model high school curriculum which contained as requisites for high school graduation a minimum of one semester each in art history and music history. Such a curriculum would fill a gap which currently exists in most schools, where the focus of arts courses in lower grades is primarily on production and performance. But attention also needs to be given to theater, dance, design, and the media arts. It is the combination of arts instruction which is essential to cultural literacy.

Secretary Bennett's recommendation for a requirement of one year of study in the arts for high school graduation parallels trends at state and district levels and goes further. Twenty-nine states now include the arts in their list of requirements for high school graduation, up from 22 states in 1984. But only nine of these make arts mandatory per se for all students (seven more do so for college-bound students), and 13 of these states require the arts only in the alternative with other subjects, such as foreign languages and computer sciences. (See Figure 1, pp. 20-21.) The number of school districts which require the arts for high school graduation requirements has, nonetheless, doubled in the past five years, from 18 percent in 1981-82 to 36 percent in 1986-87. (See Figure 8.)

THE STATE OF THE CURRICULUM IN ARTS EDUCATION

The degree of guidance in establishing learning goals in the arts varies from state to state and district to district.

At the state level, *Arts, Education and the States*, the 1985 report by the Council of Chief State School Officers, indicates that while 93 percent of state education agencies had established education goals, only one-fourth of these had included specific reference to the arts. Most states provide curriculum guides to local districts, and many of these stipulate specific competencies for specific grade levels in visual arts and music. But most of the guides are nondirective, leaving responsibility for what is actually taught to school districts, and do not deal with the arts other than the visual arts and music.

At the district level, the 1987 U.S. Department of Education survey of school districts (1987 district survey) indicates that most districts have curriculum guides that specify instructional goals in terms of student outcomes. But the availability of these guides varies by discipline and grade level. Seventy-five percent of school districts have music guides for all grade levels, but only 35 percent have them at the elementary grade level for dance, drama, and creative writing. And, while about half of the school districts have arts curriculum coordinators, only 30 percent of the districts have coordinators for dance, drama, and creative writing at the elementary level. Even in music and the visual arts, only 7 percent of the districts required competency tests for promotion to the next school grade.

Guides in Visual Arts

Arizona students are supposed to "use different kinds and qualities of lines (thick, thin, straight, curved, wavy, jagged, broken) in nonobjective composition." *Illinois* students are to "use specific lines to create a specified effect such as hard, soft, bold, gentle;" *South Dakota* grade five and six "students will use a wide variety of lines in making line drawings." *North Carolina* students are supposed to "demonstrate an understanding of the basic elements of art . . . discriminate among various kinds of line qualities . . . explore various qualities of line in her/his work . . . continue to develop an expressive use of line." In *Minnesota* "the student will identify simple line, directions of line and movement in line" and "describe expressive characteristics of lines, e.g., smooth, jagged, thick, thin, dark, light." *Kentucky* students should "discover line in art forms of the natural environment . . . of the man-made environment . . . create with the use of line."

In *Kansas,* "the student will demonstrate an understanding of the elements of design. 1. Line: . . . define and use contour line to create a shape . . . use line to interpret directional movement (vertical, horizontal, and diagonal) . . . use line to show depth or volume . . . use line to create texture." *Arkansas* students should "recognize thick, thin, long, short, straight, curved and zigzag lines. Draw a picture using a variety of lines. Create a work of art using a variety of lines with a variety of media."

Guides in Music

Alaska students are to "know how to increase skill in rhythmic movement. Perform rhythmic drills such as clapping hands, snapping fingers, or tapping feet to feel pulsation." In *Illinois,* "by the end of grade 6, students should be able to: . . . sing or play at sight music that contains stepwise motion and simple rhythm patterns." In *Texas,* "the student shall be provided opportunities to: . . . see, play, and sing simple melodic and rhythmic patterns, steady beat, beat groupings." *North Carolina* students are to "understand that rhythm patterns may be combined and performed simultaneously. Perform polyrhythms . . . Differentiate between the rhythm of the melody and that of the underlying beat . . . Perform readily either the melodic or beat rhythm." *Kansas* students should, in playing instruments, "perform increasingly complex rhythmic patterns in a variety of meters."

Source: Compiled by Dr. Brent G. Wilson, Professor of Art, Pennsylvania State University, in summer of 1987.

Problems With Current Curriculum Guides

The single greatest drawback of existing arts curricula and the guides which teachers use is their emphasis on skill development at the expense of the art form as a whole. Our review of state curriculum guides indicates that the broad learning goals stated in the guides are generally well balanced. They include (i) broadening the student's understanding of the cultural heritage of art and music; (ii) developing the student's ability to make judgments on the quality of works of art and music; (iii) developing the student's ability skillfully to perform art or music; and (iv) generating an understanding of the basic elements of visual art or music. The problem is that the specific learning objectives do not reflect the balance contained in the goals. Rather, they tend to emphasize the last goal, learning the elements of the arts forms, over study of works of art. The result is that the goals tend to be obscured in a sea of narrowly focused "skill" outcomes.

For example, many of the state visual arts guides have sections relating to *line*, but the sections tend to isolate line from other elements of visual art. Similarly, music guides will focus on developing isolated skills, such as rhythm, and ignore others. (See excerpted examples, p. 74.) Students may be able to use or identify line or rhythm, but will have little understanding of what music and art really are. Of even greater concern is the guides' failure to specify which works of music or art should be analyzed through the study of their elements.

Examples of different approaches are seen in excerpts from state guidelines in Illinois and Oklahoma (Figures 9 and 10, pp. 76-77). An example of a state guide which is better at relating goals to learning objectives is seen in an excerpt from the Georgia visual arts guide (Figure 11, p. 78).

A second problem is that media education is almost never factored into the formal K-12 curriculum. Study of the media, how they deliver information and influence attitudes, is something very few children are exposed to in school. Thus most students have no tools to develop the critical attitudes that would enable them to become discriminating viewers and listeners. While print literacy is recognized as of prime importance and English studies are basic in every school in every grade, media literacy remains untaught and unrecognized.

A third problem is that the curriculum guides are written by specialists for specialists and frequently fail to provide nonspecialist teachers with the practical information and minimum resources they need. Although the guides generally contain goal statements and long lists of objectives or competencies that students should achieve at different grade levels, they seldom outline the sequence of instruction or list works of art that might provide content and subject matter in the classroom.

Figure 9. General Goals for High School Graduates in the Visual Arts and Music

FINE ARTS
GRADE 12

STATE GOAL FOR LEARNING 1

As a result of their schooling, students will be able to understand the principal sensory, formal, technical and expressive qualities of each of the arts.

SAMPLE LEARNING OBJECTIVES FOR GOAL 1

Visual Art

By the end of GRADE 12, students, given a selected visual image, should be able to:

A1. Analyze how color, line, shape, texture and space interact in that image.

B1. Analyze how balance, rhythm, contrast, unity and variety are used in that image.

C1. Understand how skills, materials and techniques were used to produce that image.

D1. Understand how the mood, emotion, idea or value is expressed in that image.

E1. Relate personal preferences for a work of art in terms of the sensory, formal and technical qualities.

E2. Understand the ways the sensory, formal and technical qualities perceived in an art work interact to express ideas.

Music

By the end of GRADE 12, students should be able to:

F1. Analyze how tone color, pitch dynamics, texture, rhythm and tempo interact in a specified musical composition.

G1. Analyze how repetition and contrast are used to create form in a specified musical composition.

H1. Understand how skill, technique and sound production affect a musical performance.

I1. Understand how a mood, emotion, idea or value is expressed in a specified musical composition.

Source: Illinois State Board of Education, *State Goals for Learning and Sample Learning Objectives*, September 1986. p. 25. Reprinted with permission.

Figure 10. General Music Guide: Grades 7-9

General Music
Grades 7-9

The general music course should be designed to accommodate a variety of music activities. Ideally, students should pursue musical experiences they have not had the opportunity to pursue before, or choose to concentrate in an aspect of music that has special appeal. Students should be encouraged to continue musical studies throughout the secondary school years and beyond. One year of music during junior or senior high school should be required.

Performing Skills

1. Develop the ability to produce music alone and with others using the voice, environmental sounds, electronic sounds, body sounds, keyboard instruments, and folk instruments.
2. Use the instrument as a means of personal expression, and perform on a variety of musical instruments.
3. Develop performance skills through the study of idiomatic literature.
4. Perform basic chord patterns upon piano and keyboard-type instruments.

Organizing Skills

1. Experiment with the organization and manipulation of musical materials.
2. Demonstrate ability to develop and communicate original musical ideas.
3. Create, arrange and improvise melodies and accompaniments in a variety of styles.
4. Compose and improvise idiomatic literature.
5. Create music using electronic media.
6. Improvise and play by ear.

Describing Skills

1. Describe how instrumental sounds are produced.
2. Listen to, analyze and discuss the literature studied and similar literature.
3. Develop the perceptual skill and vocabulary to discuss music.
4. Study the common elements of music.
5. Develop further the ability to read and interpret music notation.

Source: Oklahoma State Department of Education, *Curriculum Review Handbook: The Arts*, June, 1985. p. 19 (as adapted from the *Visual and Performing Arts Framework for the California Public Schools*, 1982). Reprinted with permission.

Figure 11. Georgia Visual Arts Guide

D. Knowledge of History of Art and its Relationship to Other Disciplines

Study of major works, artists and movements in the student's own culture as well as other cultures, both contemporary and historical, is a fundamental part of education in the arts. In the opinion of most historians, contact with great works of art is a means of understanding human ideals and aspirations and appreciating the heroic, comic and tragic in human affairs. The history of world art furnishes us with many examples of human courage, endurance and achievement.

In achieving this goal of art instruction the student should recognize major historical periods, works, artists and styles, especially those which have had an enduring effect. It requires that students have some contact with clear, interesting writing or discourse explaining technical discoveries and historically important innovations. The student should be able to explain the reasons for critical acclaim of selected figures, monuments or works as superior examples summing up the spirit of the age in which they occur. Such activities can be supplemented and made more memorable by visits to actual collections or museums, to famous architectural sites and monuments — the visits to be followed up by discussion and research. Similarly, visits by museum curators or gallery owners, art historians or private collectors who discuss the special nature of their collections, is another important avenue for increasing student understanding of the historical dimensions of the visual arts.

Finally, articles, lectures or discussions that explore and explain relationships between particular art movements and other historical or sociological events should be offered whenever possible. Understanding the connections between art styles and life styles from different cultures and historical epochs is the aim of instruction and student inquiry.

Eugene Delacroix (French, 1798-1863)
***Delteil*, 116 from "Hamlet" series, 1843**
(lithograph, second state)
The High Museum of Art, Atlanta

Source: Division of Curriculum Services, Office of Instructional Services, Georgia Department of Education, *Visual Arts Education Guidelines, K-12*, 1982, p. 21. Reprinted with permission.

A fourth problem is that the curriculum guides tend to replicate existing guides and ignore the highly regarded work of American arts curriculum theorists and researchers. The 19th-century system of teaching visual art through segmentation of the elements and principles of design (line, color, shape, texture, balance, opposition) still prevails in most visual arts instruction today, even though it ignores such vital elements as theme, subject matter, symbol, style, and expressiveness. Similar examples can be found in music curriculum guides and, to a lesser degree, in a few curriculum guides that have been prepared for dance, drama, and the other art forms.

There is little interaction between the arts education theoreticians and researchers and the arts curriculum coordinators and teachers. The curriculum coordinators are the ones who more often than not are called on to develop state and local arts curriculum guides, but they lack theoretical expertise, time and financing, often having no alternative but to borrow from guides used by other states or school districts. Conversely, the theoreticians attain academic promotion and prestige for their lectures and publication of academic papers rather than for actual classroom implementation of their work. The theories of arts education should be more than subjects of academic debate.

DEVELOPING RESOURCE MATERIALS FOR TEACHING THE ARTS

There are only a few visual arts textbooks that strike a balance between making art and studying art, and even these are not widely used (by less than 5 percent of teachers according to one editor). An example of a teacher's edition of a visual arts textbook by Laura Chapman is seen in Figure 12, pp. 82-83.

Visual arts teachers often assign students to do a painting of a collection of bottles, pots, and dried weeds without any reference to the tradition of still-life painting. Further, unlike music textbooks which are well funded, visual arts textbooks are generally produced by individual writers working on their own time.

Curriculum resources for creative writing are sometimes found in language arts textbooks, but creative writing as an art form does not receive much special attention. In theater, there are resource materials for teachers, but no textbook series for students. In dance, new resource materials have become available in the last 20 years in "creative movement" and "creative dance." No standard instructional materials exist in the design and media arts.

On the other hand, comprehensive and detailed instructional resource materials have been available in music for over a hundred years. Music teachers in elementary and middle schools can choose from three major sets of music textbooks. These include teachers' editions with well over a hundred lessons as parts of major units of instruction on contemporary, traditional, American and folk, classical, and holiday music. The lessons involve concepts (such as rhythm and melody) and skills (such as listening, analyzing, reading, creating, and performing music). Unfortunately, many school districts do not spend the money to acquire these excellent texts.

Music textbook publishers invest substantial resources and employ large numbers of researchers and experts in developing music text series. (See following box for a good example of a music textbook publisher's editorial process.) Excellent examples of teachers' editions of two music textbook series are seen in Figures 13 and 14, pp. 84-87.

Developing a Music Textbook Series

Silver, Burdett & Ginn Co. employs eleven music editors full time. For a series called *World of Music*, the Company spent millions of dollars; employed a dozen music educators from select colleges and public schools as writers; conducted a teachers' summer workshop; asked 19 writers to develop teachers' handbooks; involved over 100 artists in executing the illustrations; used advisors responsive to minority student needs; and, when the series was completed, used 21 "critic readers" and more than 50 teachers to test the book in the field. In order to be responsive to the market, the publisher sent detailed questionnaires to 1300 individuals randomly selected from among the users of the current series.

The new series reflects the latest trends in music education yet retains links with past editions. Each of the nine books of this series includes approximately 110 songs (folk, traditional, seasonal and holiday) and deals with the social, cultural and historical aspects of music; it also deals with refinement of performance and music reading skills and the structural elements of music. Instructional materials accompanying the textbooks include suggested activities involving other school subjects. The series includes student activity sheets and tests; 93 records with some 900 songs, including standard selections leased by record companies and some commissioned in the past from composers such as Humperdinck, Rachmaninoff, Copland, and Hindemith; and interviews with composers including Barber, Copland, Rodgers, Schuman and Stravinsky.

Source: Interview notes by Dr. Brent G. Wilson, Professor of Art, Pennsylvania State University, in summer of 1987.

Before the invention and widespread use of recordings, printed music was a necessary component of instrumental and vocal instruction, establishing a tradition that continues to this day. In the other arts, however, until recently it has been assumed that the only necessary instructional materials were imagination, bodies and voices, and ample supplies of paint, pencils, and clay. Perhaps the current movement toward teaching important works of art will stimulate publication and use of texts and resources that integrate ideas and concepts with creation and performance.

It is time to go beyond assumptions about the arts curriculum and pose and answer the key questions.

CRITICAL ISSUES IN THE ARTS CURRICULUM

- What should be the balance between studying specific works of art which tell us about civilization and America's artistic heritage and studying the basic skills of creation and performance?

- Which works of art and what artists should be known and understood by every elementary, middle, and high school student?

- What should the balance be between study of Western art and the arts of other cultures and civilizations, among the various art disciplines, and between "classical" art, folk art, and popular art?

- What should be the balance between studying works of art for their aesthetic qualities, as pure form, and the study of works of art as narratives about people, history, society, and of ideas, values, beliefs?

- What should be the balance between curricula and resources designed to teach the arts as separate subjects and curricula and resources aimed at integrating arts study into other academic subjects?

- What kind of curriculum should be designed for students with artistic talent?

Figure 12. Excerpt from a Teacher's Edition of a Visual Art Textbook.

Preparation

- pencils
- drawing paper, 1 sheet per student

Note: Preview the activity. You might wish to try drawing steps yourself first so that the lesson will go more smoothly. This lesson is intended to strengthen students' intuitive understanding of perspective and visual rhythms.

Objectives

Vocabulary: rhythms, overlap
Students will:

a) perceive in two works of art (paintings) how visual rhythms are created by overlapping and repeating shapes, lines and colors.
b) appreciate that overlapping shapes can be arranged to suggest near and distant space in artwork.
c) create a drawing of a crowd of people and attempt to create a visual rhythm by overlapping the figures.

44

Drawing
Crowds of People

A

Jose Clemente Orozco, Zapatistas, 1931. Oil on canvas, 45 × 55" (114 × 140 cm). Collection, The Museum of Modern Art, New York (Anonymous gift).

José Orozco's painting tells about a leader of the Mexican people. Artists say that Orozco's painting has visual rhythms. The rhythms are created by repeated lines and shapes.

Picture B shows how the artist overlapped the main shapes. Overlap means some shapes are in front of others. The overlapped shapes help create a visual rhythm in the painting.

B

92

Exploration

about 6 minutes

1. Work through the text on the left-hand page. Focus on picture A, a painting by José Orozco, and help students perceive and kinesthetically feel the visual rhythms. Have students make short rhythmic gestures which match the long scarfs (inverted U-shapes), curved hats, swords and the long sloping lines of the marching figures. Note how the four hats of horseback riders alternate in position. Explain that the painting shows a group of Mexican leaders on horseback leading people who want freedom.
2. Focus on diagram B. Help students see how the simple overlapped shapes represent near and distant figures as seen in picture A. Note how the diagrammed shapes also create curved visual rhythms that seem to move toward the left of the picture.
3. Work through the text on the right-hand page. Use the same basic procedures. Have students identify repeated elements and gesture some of the angular and vertical rhythms in picture C, a painting by Jacob Lawrence. Using picture D, help the students see how the figures near the bottom of Lawrence's painting overlap the street. Note how marching figures overlap and form rows.
4. Read about the activity. Explain that you will help students understand how to begin their drawing.

Activity

about 25 minutes

1. Distribute the materials. Offer step-by-step guidance. Ask everyone to lightly draw three or four lines across the width of their paper. The lines might be wavy, wide zigzags or long, lazy "S" shapes turned sideways. Explain these rhythm lines will help to create a visual rhythm in the drawing.
2. Second, have students draw oval shapes which will represent heads of people standing side-by-side. Have students draw three or four large ovals

Source: Laura H. Chapman, *Discover Art* (Teacher's Edition, Grade 4), Davis Publications, Worcester, MA., 1985. pp. 92-93. Reprinted with permission.

C

Jacob Lawrence, *The Parade*, 16¼ × 20⅛" (41 × 51 cm). Hirshhorn Museum and Sculpture Garden, Smithsonian Institution, Washington, D.C.

Jacob Lawrence's painting of a parade also has visual rhythms. What lines and shapes help create rhythms?

See if you can draw a crowd of people. Draw several people first. Draw them quite large. Then draw more people behind the first ones.

If you can, plan your picture so it has visual rhythms.

D

93

so the chin of the head (oval) touches the rhythm line near the bottom of the drawing. The rest of the figure and details will be added later.

3. Third, have students draw smaller oval shapes for heads so the chin line touches the next rhythm line. Some of the ovals can be partially drawn so they look like they are behind the first ones. (For now, leave other rhythm lines as they are.)
4. Now have students add the facial details, neck and body to their first ovals near the bottom of the paper. When these additions are complete, have them draw faces, necks and so on to complete second row of figures.
5. Hold up some of the drawings that are in progress. Suggest that students continue to draw other people along the remaining rhythm lines. Note that rhythm lines might be used in other ways — to draw trees, mountains, clouds, or city skyline.

Extensions

Effort and Concentration: If drawings from this lesson are quite good, provide time and materials so students can color or paint the drawings, creating additional visual rhythms by repeating colors and adding patterns.

Cleanup

about 1 minute

1. Collect the artwork after the evaluation.
2. Have students check floor for supplies. Collect and put away art materials.

Evaluation

about 4 minutes

1. Ask volunteers to hold up their work. Discuss use of overlapping and smaller shapes to suggest near and distant figures. Note how different visual rhythms have been established by use of wavy, zigzag or other lines.
2. Refer to objectives a–c to review the major points in the lesson and to evaluate results.

Figure 13. Excerpt from a Teacher's Edition of a Music Textbook

Lesson Plan

Focus Listening to music for solo instrument and orchestra

Concept Objectives, p. xxiv

Materials Record 1B, Band 2

Vocabulary concerto

1. Tell students they will hear some music that was written by a composer who was born in the same year as a famous American president. Then play a little of the Haydn piece (about 20 seconds or so).

2. Put Haydn and his music in a historical perspective.
• Franz Joseph Haydn and George Washington were both born in 1732.
• It is entirely possible that during his lifetime, Washington heard some of Haydn's music at informal musical gatherings in his home at Mount Vernon or at concert halls in Philadelphia and New York.

3. Play the entire piece and ask students to listen for the general feeling, or mood, of the music.
• What adjectives can you use to describe the mood of the music? (Most students will agree that the music is lively, bright, vigorous, energetic, and cheerful.)
• What qualities in the music help to create this lively mood? (Fast tempo, fairly loud dynamic level, many fast notes played briskly, rapid scale patterns that sweep upward and downward)

4. Have students read the definition of a concerto (kuhn-CHERH-toh) in the text on p. 28 in their book.
• Identify a *movement* as one of several separate sections of a longer composition.

A Concerto by Haydn

A concerto is a composition written for solo instrument with orchestra. You will hear the last movement of a concerto by Franz Joseph Haydn. What solo instrument do you hear in this piece? Listen for the parts where the solo instrument plays alone and where the orchestra plays alone.

Concerto in D Major, Movement 3 .... Haydn

This little folk-dance tune is heard many times throughout the piece. Sometimes it is played by the piano, and at other times, by the orchestra.

28

Special Resources

Listening Lessons Haydn's *Concerto in D Major* is the first of six major listening lessons presented in this book. Through these lessons, students are introduced to music that represents various styles and periods of composition. It is hoped that students will develop a familiarity with the selections that are presented in these lessons—a familiarity that will lead to a deeper understanding and a heightened appreciation of the music. But for this to happen, students must be given an opportunity to hear each selection many times. From time to time, a review of the music will be suggested to enhance other lessons. In addition, it is hoped that you will take every opportunity to have students hear these selections again.

Related Literature Students may enjoy the following book:
• *The Boy Who Loved Music* by David Lasker (Viking)—Karl is a young horn player in the prince's orchestra, which is directed by Haydn. When Haydn's new symphony surprises the prince, the musicians achieve their desire of leaving the summer castle and returning to Vienna.

Source: J. Beethoven, et al., *World of Music* (Teacher's Edition, Grade 5), Silver, Burdett & Ginn, Morristown, N.J., 1988, pp. 28-29. Reprinted with permission.

Listen for the short notes that decorate the music. These short notes are called *grace notes*.

Here are two other themes to listen for.

Franz Joseph Haydn
(1732–1809)

Haydn was born in a small village in Austria. His father made wheels for carriages, and his mother was a cook in the household of a count. When Haydn was a little boy, he would pretend to play the violin with two pieces of wood as he listened to his mother singing the folk songs of the area. It is possible that one of the songs she sang was the little dance tune Haydn used in his *Concerto in D Major*.

In 1761 a wealthy Austrian nobleman named Esterhazy hired Haydn to write music for his private orchestra. In those days, every castle had its own band of professional musicians. For 30 years, Haydn lived at the Esterhazy castle. Although a musician living in a nobleman's house was nothing more than a servant, Haydn never minded. He was a simple man who was grateful for the opportunity to compose and perform music.

29

Extension

1. When the recording is played another time, have students listen especially for the interplay between the solo instrument and the orchestra. Can the students hear when the piano plays alone? When the orchestra plays alone?

2. On another day, focus attention on the themes that are notated on pp. 28 and 29 in the Student Text.
- If possible, play each theme on the piano.
- Have students clap the melodic rhythm of theme 1. Call attention to the characteristic rhythm pattern that students will hear all through the Haydn piece.

- Have students clap the melodic rhythm of theme 3. Compare the melodic rhythm of themes 1 and 3.

- Compare the way in which the tones move in theme 3 (generally downward) with the way in which tones move in theme 4 (generally upward).

Note: Being aware of what is happening in smaller segments of a piece of music will help students hear more of what is going on when they listen to the entire piece.

The Father of the Symphony Haydn's contribution to music was more than his 104 symphonies, more than his 82 string quartets, more than his 52 piano sonatas and hundreds of other compositions. Haydn's contribution to music was his ability to sum up all the styles of music that came before him and to set certain standards for various forms. Haydn is often called the Father of the Symphony.

Haydn's active musical life spanned many years. During those years his music changed as he experimented with instrumental combinations, form, and major and minor modes. The music itself is considered *classical* in that it is *absolute music*—music that does not depend upon art, literature, or any extramusical idea for its meaning. The meaning is in the music itself.

Haydn died in 1809. He had been a friend to Mozart, a teacher to Beethoven, and an inspiration to everyone who came in contact with him.

Figure 14. Excerpt from a Teacher's Edition of a Music Textbook

THE IMPORTANCE OF REPETITION

Purpose: To develop the concept that repetition is necessary to achieve balance in form.

Materials: Textbook.

Motivation: Look around the room to find examples of balance through repetition. (Perhaps the arrangement of lighting fixtures, windows, or floor tiles.) Look at the human figure to discover the balance created by two arms, legs, ears, and eyes.

Exploration: Have the children:

1. Study the illustrations on the page to find examples of balance through repetition.
2. Read the art text.
3. Look at the notation of "Sourwood Mountain" on p. 121. Identify repeated parts. [*Line 2 of the music is an exact repetition of line 1; line 4 is the same as line 3. There is repetition of chord patterns in lines 1 and 2, 3 and 4. There is word repetition in the last half of each line.*]

Extension: The students might find other pictures that illustrate balance through repetition.

Desired Responses: The students should be able to verbally identify balance as created through repetition in art and in music notation.

Seagram Building

Robert Doisneau from Rapho Guillumette Pictures

Balance in musical form

Repetition helps give balance to music. There are many kinds of musical repetition.

The pictures above show two types of structures. Each structure looks like one unit. Each structure appears to be balanced. Visual balance helps unify a work. How do you think balance is achieved in each of these structures?

120

Related Arts The principle of balance is one of the structural concepts artists use in making art. There are two types of balance. *Formal balance* is found when two sides of an object or design are the same on each side of a center line. *Informal balance* occurs when the parts on each side of a center line differ, but where they look balanced. The cathedral of Notre Dame in Paris and the modern office building are both examples of formal balance.

Curriculum Correlation Explain to the students that "Sourwood Mountain" is sung during folk dances in the Appalachian Mountain region of the United States. Ask the students to locate this area on a map [*Mountain chain extending from Canada to Alabama*]

Have the students do research and find the reasons why people do folk dancing. Here is some of the interesting data that the students might find:

In America and in Europe, folk dances usually were danced in the country. They developed as the chief form of amuse-

Source: M. V. Marsh et al., *Macmillan Music: The Spectrum of Music with Related Arts* (Teacher's Annotated Edition, Level 5), Macmillan, New York, N.Y., 1983, pp. 120-121. Reprinted with permission.

Where do you find repetition in "Sourwood Mountain"?

Sourwood Mountain

Appalachian Folk Song

F Bb C7 F C7 F

1. Chick-en crow-in' on Sour-wood Moun-tain, Hey de-ing dang did-dle al-ly day.
2. My true love's a blue-eyed dai - sy

F Bb C7 F C7 F

So man-y pret-ty girls I can't count them. Hey de-ing dang did-dle al-ly day.
If I don't get her I'll go cra - zy,

F Dm F C7 F

My true love she lives in Letch-er, Hey de-ing dang did-dle al-ly day.
My true love lives in the hol - low,

F Dm F C7 F

She won't come and I won't fetch her, Hey de-ing dang did-dle al-ly day.
She won't come and I won't fol - low,

Look at the four phrases of this song. Each line is a phrase. Now look at the groups of letters below. Each letter stands for a phrase. Which of the following groups of letters shows the phrase form of this song?

A A B B   A B A B   A B A C

K d' ls mrd l, s,   Reinforce: tiritiri tiri ti tim-ri patterns.

121

ment for people who had little else in the way of entertainment. On holidays and feast days the people gathered together in their best clothes to dance.

Other people do folk dancing for other reasons. Dancing has been part of the religious life of some people. The dances of the East Indies are temple dances. The dances of some peoples are designed to please their gods or to petition them, such as rain dancing in dry seasons.

EXPLORING REPETITION

Purpose: To explore repetition of phrases. To identify the phrase form of the song.

Materials: Textbook, recording, autoharp or ukulele, resonator bells or piano, MusicCenter 33, 34.

Motivation: Locate the Appalachian Mountain region on a map. Discuss the purpose of the song. [*For fun and dancing*] Say the repeated nonsense words at the end of each phrase.

Exploration: Have the students:

1. Read the words of the song to find the humor.
2. Look at the last measure of each line. Play an A on the resonator bells or piano and sing the measure: A, A, G, G, F.
3. Learn to sing the entire song.
4. Accompany the song on the autoharp or ukulele. Observe again that the sequences of chords are alike in lines 1 and 2, 3 and 4.
5. Read the text and answer the question. [*The phrase form is A A B B.*]
6. Create a circle dance for the song using repeated patterns to show the phrase form.

Extension: The students might also create a simple percussion composition in A A B B form.

Desired Responses: The students should be able to identify the phrase form of this and other A A B B songs and create a dance in this form.

Music Background A phrase in music is comparable to a sentence in speech. It is a natural division of the melodic line. A phrase usually includes 2, 4, or 8 measures and is sometimes indicated by a phrase mark (or curved line). A phrase mark should not be confused with a tie or a slur mark. A tie only connects two notes of the same pitch. A slur mark is used when two notes are sung on one syllable.

RECOMMENDATIONS

1. Arts education should provide all students with a sense of the arts in civilization, of creativity in the artistic process, of the vocabularies of artistic communication, and of the critical elements necessary to making informed choices about the products of the arts.

2. State education agencies and local school districts should adopt and implement explicit policies to make such arts education a sequential part of the basic curriculum for all students in grades K-12. These policies should define the curriculum to include each of the arts (dance, design, literature and creative writing, the media arts, music, opera and musical theater, theater, and the visual arts) and provide for instruction in history and critical analysis as well as production and performance. Most important, the policies should define a core of subject content and skills in the arts which all students would be required to achieve, and provide for a selection of required courses in relation to optional courses in the basic curriculum. It is particularly important that the policies include provision for the all-pervasive design and media arts. The policies should also provide for time, money, and qualified personnel to develop comprehensive and sequential curricula, instruction based on the curricula, and testing of student achievement and evaluation of school programs. To this end:

   A. State education agencies and school districts should identify, and achieve consensus on, the minimum knowledge and skills (in terms of student learning outcomes) that would satisfy state or district-mandated high school graduation requirements.

   B. Elementary schools should consider providing arts instruction, exclusive of English studies, for approximately 15 percent of the school week consistent with the aims of professional arts education associations. Four-and-a-half hours of arts instruction in a 30-hour elementary school week is fairly minimal if students are to gain a sense of the arts as described above.

   C. Junior high and middle schools (grades 6 through 8) should require *all* students to take arts instruction, exclusive of English studies, for at least 15 percent of the school year (the average for the majority of students in grades 7 and 8 is estimated at 17 percent). These requirements might be fulfilled through survey courses, through study of at least two of the arts, or through instruction integrated with other academic courses. The curriculum should specifically require study of the design and media arts, and teachers should be trained to teach these subjects.

D. High schools should require all students satisfactorily to complete two full years (or two Carnegie units) involving the arts (not as an alternative to courses like foreign languages or computer sciences) in order to receive a graduation diploma. The purpose is to provide *all* high school students with a basic sense of the history and vocabularies of the arts and their significance in society. This purpose might be achieved either through arts courses per se or through making the arts integral parts of other courses. High schools and school systems will have to certify which of their courses meet this purpose. They may also wish to consider a seven-period day in accommodating these and other increased requirements.

E. High schools should also offer optional introductory, intermediate, and advanced courses in each of the arts so that those interested and/or talented in an art form might be able to pursue that interest and talent.

F. State education agencies and school districts should engage knowledgeable experts to coordinate arts curriculum development and evaluation. The experts should work closely with teachers and school administrators, and with theoreticians and researchers, in order to employ the best available thinking in this effort. The experts should also engage the resources of artists, arts, and cultural institutions, teacher-training institutions, and commercial producers of classroom materials.

G. State and local education budgets should provide for making appropriate arts materials (e.g., textbooks, teacher manuals, and audio-visual aids) available to students and teachers. Where such materials do not exist, state education agencies and school districts should collaborate in developing incentives for their production.

The Case for Testing and Evaluation in the Arts

What do American students learn in their arts classes? Unfortunately, there is little data at either the national or state level, and even less at local levels, on which to base an answer. Nowhere in the country is there any systematic, comprehensive, and formal assessment of student achievement in the arts. Nor is there any such assessment of the effectiveness of arts programs, either at the school or district level.

Testing is a fact of life in reading, language, math, history, and science. Why not in the arts?

UNIQUE PROBLEMS IN TESTING STUDENT ACHIEVEMENT IN THE ARTS

The first problem confronting testing in the arts is the lack of standardized curricula, texts, and resource materials which could provide a standard base of knowledge against which to test across the many different local school districts. While other areas of the curriculum achieve standardization through use of such materials, they either do not exist or are seldom used in the arts, except in music. Instruction in the visual arts is so idiosyncratic that even in small school districts teachers often cannot agree on standard drawing and design tasks or on history of art questions to test student achievement district-wide.

A second problem for testing and assessment in arts education stems from the nature of the arts and the character of arts instruction. Reading and spelling can be assessed by standardized multiple-choice achievement tests. But creative writing can only be tested by determining whether the student has written a good poem or short story. This requires agreement on plot structure, setting, character development, style, and expressiveness of language as critical elements of short-story writing and on standards for judging achievement in these elements. It also requires expert scorers who might take a half-hour or more to analyze the short story of a single student, whereas an entire battery of multiple-choice questions on reading and spelling can be posed to thousands of students and machine scored in minutes. Analysis and assessment of student achievement in other art forms can be equally complex.

Third, arts educators are themselves divided as to whether testing in the arts is a good idea. Some believe that testing should be conducted in the arts in the same way as for any other school subject; others say that meaningful testing in the arts is impossible. And some suggest that testing may actually have a negative effect on the way the arts are taught.

PRECEDENTS FOR TESTING IN THE ARTS

National Evaluation

While standardized tests are rarely used in the arts, the National Assessment of Educational Progress (NAEP) has created a national precedent for arts testing. Initiated by the U.S. Office of Education in 1969, NAEP seeks to determine how well students across the country, of different ages and different social and economic backgrounds, achieve the major goals and objectives of American education. Students ages nine, 13, and 17 (or grades four, eight, and 12) are asked to respond to a variety of questions, tasks, and exercises on subjects generally taught in schools. NAEP reports publicly on the student responses and interprets the results.

NAEP's initial plans, developed during the 1960's, included art and music among the first 10 school subjects selected for study. Creative writing was also assessed as a part of general writing, but plans to assess dance and theater were never developed.

In 1971-72, and again in 1978-79, a nationally representative sample of students was asked to play, perform, and improvise pieces of music; read standard musical notation; analyze musical selections; respond to questions about the history of music; express attitudes toward music; and make judgments about the merit of musical selections.

In 1974-75 and 1978-79, a similar sample was assessed regarding the visual arts. (The visual arts testing was delayed because there had been little previous testing in this area and most of the tests had to be invented specially for NAEP.) Students were asked to recognize and analyze the features of art works; indicate the degree to which they valued experiences with art; demonstrate their ability to produce works of art with specific features; tell what they knew about the history of art; and justify judgments about the merit and quality of works of art.

The item writers of both the art and music assessments were told to be innovative in developing test procedures and to ignore constraints of cost, time, administration, and scoring. Most important, they were not asked to restrict tasks to those that could be tested in multiple-choice formats scorable by machine. Although many innovative testing procedures were developed, most were set aside before the art and music assessments were undertaken because they were considered too difficult to administer and too expensive and time-consuming to analyze. Nonetheless, the National Assessment did result in an examination that included questions that went beyond a machine-scored format.

While all testing that goes beyond machine-scored formats poses similar problems, the irony is that dependency on machine-scored testing may in the long run prove more expensive, since it is seldom able to elicit a sense of what the student knows and, most important, can do.

Nonetheless, the NAEP assessments in art and music represent the most systematic evaluation efforts undertaken in these two subjects to date. Unfortunately, although the original NAEP plan provided for a new assessment of art and music at least once every six years, none has been conducted since 1979. While the results of a large portion of the arts assessments were published, some data from the 1978-79 art assessment still remain unscored, unanalyzed, and unreported.

A 1987 study initiated by the U.S. Department of Education (known as the Alexander-James report) called for regular assessments of what it called the "core curriculum" — defined as reading, writing, and literacy; mathematics, science, and technology; and history, geography, and civics. The report noted, however, that music, art, and literature, while once a regular part of the assessment, should be the subject of "special assessments from time to time in response to the expressed needs of the public and the educational community."

The U.S. Department of Education asked the National Academy of Education to comment on the recommendations in the Alexander-James report. In a summary of the Academy response (also presented in *The Nation's Report Card*, the publication featuring the Alexander-James report and the Academy response), Robert Glaser wrote the following:

> The NAEP needs to expand its areas of testing to remind the nation that schooling involves much more than just competencies in reading, writing, and mathematics. The Alexander-James report recommends that science, history, civics, and geography be added to the core assessment. The report also suggests possible future assessments in social studies and the arts. We would like to endorse the humanities. Their importance has been neglected for too long. Here, more than anywhere else in the curriculum, is where those fundamental human qualities mentioned above are the subject matter of instruction. *We repeat that what is assessed tends to become what the community values.** Thus it seems critical that the assessment direct attention toward the fullness of the human experience. (p.54)
>
> *italics added

It is important to note that NAEP has a limited function. At its inception, there was concern in some quarters that it could lead to development of a national curriculum, a violation of our tradition of local school control. Some feared that it might reflect negatively on individual states or school districts. Consequently, the Assessment's findings are reported only for the four major regions of the country and their usefulness is limited.

The Reagan Administration has proposed expansion of NAEP to provide for state-by-state comparisons. If the NAEP expansion were extended to the arts, it would permit national and state-level assessment and comparisons.

As it now stands, if states and school districts are to use assessment data as a basis for school improvement, they will need to develop their own assessment programs. A good assessment program would force school districts and states to determine which aspects of the arts should be required knowledge so that high school graduates will be culturally literate American citizens. The National Assessment cannot now do this since it does not apply to every school district and every student.

State Evaluation

Three states—Connecticut, Minnesota, and Wisconsin—have modeled their arts assessment programs after NAEP, taking a selection of music and art items from the latter and comparing their state scores with national results. While this is a highly commendable undertaking, the three states have used only NAEP's multiple-choice questions, avoiding assessment of student achievement in the areas of art-making and performance. Furthermore, the three states did not develop test items based specifically on their own curricula, thus missing an opportunity to obtain the kind of specific information that would have allowed them to use the results of the assessments to make improvements in their schools.

The 1985 report by the Council of Chief State School Officers, *Arts, Education and the States,* reported that 10 states used statewide or standardized testing in the arts and that a number of others were developing plans to do so. But most such testing is limited to one or two subject areas, usually art or music, and in certain cases is done randomly.

As things stand now, testing in the arts is extremely difficult for most states, mainly because there is little agreement on what skills and information should be required of students, and at what levels. There are few models. If every state and local school district had to assume full responsibility for developing testing and evaluation procedures for each regular school subject, as is now the case for the arts, there would probably be little testing even in subjects like math and science which are easier to test than the arts.

School District Evaluation

Although most states have mandated arts curriculum guidelines to be followed by all their local school districts, none has yet systematically tested to determine whether or not the guideline goals are being achieved. The U.S. Department of Education's 1987 survey of school districts reveals that fewer than 7 percent of school districts use district-wide competency tests in the arts to promote students from grade to grade.

State curriculum goals and objectives in the arts are often modified at the school district level, and the instructional practices and content of local arts programs are often so varied that standardized state testing is not feasible. In addition, local school districts are generally unable to develop their own tests because they lack staff with the necessary expertise. These are problems that the arts consultants, who are employed by most state departments of education, need to address.

There needs to be a national effort to develop testing and evaluation plans, procedures, and test items in the arts that could be adapted for state and local use. Needless to say, such an effort would have to be carefully guided to assure that it does not result in a narrowing of the arts curriculum to content that is easily tested.

Project Zero (founded in 1967 as a part of the Harvard University Graduate School of Education) is collaborating with the Educational Testing Service and the Pittsburgh school system to develop ways to assess student achievement in the arts. The Educational Testing Service provides the College Board with technical expertise in developing the various tests known as the College Boards. The Project Zero approach to arts education emphasizes symbolic literacies, stressing that arts education must be cognitive as well as affective and include problem-finding and solving and decision-making. Project Zero also believes that arts education can be documented and evaluated objectively, though in different ways than other basic subjects.

THE ARGUMENTS FOR AND AGAINST TESTING

For

- For the arts to be considered legitimate and basic school subjects, student achievement in arts courses must be assessed as in other courses. Without test and assessment data, we lack information from which to evaluate the quality of arts instruction programs. If we tested higher-order skills in the arts, we would work harder to help students achieve them.

- What is to be tested will be taught; what is not tested is less likely to be taught.

- Testing can provide the information necessary to curriculum development and instructional reform in the arts.

- Much about the arts can be tested without great expense. For example, knowledge of art history, which is as vital to cultural literacy as political and economic history, can be tested in the same way as knowledge of political or economic history. Although testing of art history cannot test creation and performance skills, it can assess basic familiarity with artistic achievements and thus measure a student's knowledge of those building blocks of cultural literacy which are basic to his or her understanding of civilization.

Against

- Artistic creation and performance cannot be assessed through the multiple-choice, "right or wrong" testing methods usually employed in schools. (Nor, it should be noted, can multiple-choice questions in science or mathematics test a student's sophisticated understanding and capacity for invention in those areas.)

- If the tests are narrow and superficial, then the teaching may become narrow and superficial.

- Nonstandardized arts curricula make it nearly impossible to develop standardized tests useful to an entire school system, let alone a state or the nation.

- Few arts education professionals have the expertise needed to develop meaningful arts tests.

Why the Endowment Supports Testing

The need to measure individual progress toward curricular goals and objectives and to evaluate the relative effectiveness of different programs in achieving these goals and objectives is as valid for the arts as for any other subject. Without the information provided by testing, it is impossible to judge whether or not arts education programs are as effective as they should be, or to identify those teaching practices that should be continued and those that should be eliminated. Further, without testing, objectives for student achievement will lack specificity.

The Advanced Placement Program of the College Board has established an effective program for testing and evaluating the work of the most advanced high school art and music students.

Further, and more important, the Dutch experience with standardized testing in the arts of all high school students shows that the development of such testing in the Netherlands had the effect of increasing the visibility and seriousness of the arts curriculum as basic schooling. What was tested became what was important.

At the same time, we agree that in the arts as in other fields, too much testing today measures quantifiable low-level skills rather than significant knowledge and understanding of the essential subject matter. Arts education must be tested and evaluated, but this must be done qualitatively as well as quantitatively. Those who evaluate the quality of student work through portfolios, performances, and analyses of historical works, must themselves be sufficiently expert to make good judgments. Testing must involve the content of the arts as well as measurable, specific skills. It must also assess the students' understanding of the historical context and cultural significance of works of art.

The Advanced Placement Arts Tests: A Possible Model

The Advanced Placement Program of the College Board has established a program for testing and evaluating the work of the most advanced art and music students in the nation's high schools.

In the visual arts studio portion of this program, students work for a year to prepare general or drawing portfolios for a team of evaluators selected from a national group of high school and college art teachers. Requirements are determined by a development committee of artists and visual arts teachers from colleges and universities. Evaluation of the portfolios lasts six days — with three readers making independent judgments of the overall quality of the portfolio, at least two readers rating the breadth of the student's accomplishment, and two more independently ranking the student's thematic area of concentration. In 1987, over 2,300 participated in this evaluation program.

In order to give future students an idea of what is expected of them, the Advanced Placement Program provides Advanced Placement visual art students and teachers with reports containing color reproductions of studio portfolios submitted in previous years as well as examples of themes and ideas selected by previous examinees for their portfolios. The program also provides students and teachers with art history and music examinations used in previous years. The examinations in effect provide the basis for teacher development of Advanced Placement courses to prepare the students for the tests.

In art history, students take a three-hour examination based on a college-level full year introduction to Western art. Sixty minutes are allotted to multiple-choice questions; sixty minutes to short essays based on questions about slides of works of art; and sixty minutes to two thirty-minute essays.

In music, students may take examinations in either Music Theory or Listening and Literature. Each examination is 120 minutes long, with a balance between multiple choice and essay questions. Both include taped musical selections. In the music theory examination, students are, for example, given a printed example of a melodic phrase and asked "to compose a second melodic phrase, four to six measures long, that is a logical continuation of the first four measures but avoids exact repetition."

Although the Advanced Placement examination is now used only for the most able art and music students, the model it provides could be adopted by almost any school, school system, or state.

Testing and Curriculum Reform: Art and Music in the Netherlands

The usual practice is for a curriculum to be developed first, then implemented, and finally tested in terms of student achievement. The Dutch did it the other way around; they started with the tests. Revised curricula, new teaching resource materials, and changes in instructional practices followed. In the Netherlands, curriculum reform in the arts was in effect brought about through design of the tests.

Before 1968, when art and music became mandatory subjects in Dutch secondary schools, there was little information as to what students learned in courses in drawing and painting, crafts, music, and textile arts. Following the inclusion of art and music as required subjects, a number of arts teachers and school headmasters sought to have these subjects become part of the national system of secondary examinations that determine student qualification for university. In 1976, the arts were granted examination status, despite arguments that they should not be given such importance and that standardized syllabuses and examinations were inappropriate in the arts. Testing was not forced on the teachers but achieved through representative committees of teachers formed to work with examination specialists at the National Institute for Education Measurement (CITO).

The advent of examination items in the arts encouraged Dutch teachers to develop a highly specific and comprehensive curriculum. While Dutch art teachers had previously given lip service to teaching art history and critical analysis, the new examinations, coupled with media coverage of the exam results, forced the lip service to become reality.

The visual arts examinations assess student achievement in the creation and analysis of works of art and the history of art. In the studio portion of the examination, students are given a predetermined topic and 28 school days to produce a portfolio of working drawings, notes, and a major project that is graded by the students' teachers and by outside examiners.

The goal of the Dutch examinations is to have the students analyze art and music from the standpoint of style, meaning, and expressive character, not to acquire rote knowledge. The results of the examinations, which are released to the public through the media, are of interest to the average Dutch citizen and important to the ongoing dialogue on curriculum development.

RECOMMENDATIONS

1. As in other subjects, students should be tested in the arts and their art work evaluated in order to determine what they have learned, and arts education programs should be evaluated to determine their effectiveness.

2. State departments of education, local school districts and schools should identify, implement, and evaluate procedures to test student achievement and evaluate arts education programs on a comparative basis. To this end:

   A. Each school district should implement a comprehensive testing program in the arts based on the district's arts curriculum. The program should address creation, performance, history, critical analysis, and the place of the arts in society, and use both quantitative and qualitative measures to determine whether the student is achieving the curriculum's learning objectives.

   B. Each school district should implement an evaluation program which assesses the merit of the curriculum, adherence to it, the adequacy of resources allocated to implement it, and the level of student achievement.

   C. Each state education agency should develop evaluation procedures to evaluate district and school arts programs on a comparative basis in terms of state arts education goals.

   D. Each state education agency should provide technical assistance to school districts to help them develop student testing and program evaluation procedures.

3. The U.S. Department of Education and the National Endowment for the Arts should work together to restore to the National Assessment of Educational Progress assessments in visual art, music, and literature. The NAEP writing assessment should include creative writing. Before the next NAEP reauthorization, methods for assessing theater, dance, the design arts, and media arts should be developed, including development of prototype questions. Remaining data from the 1979 visual art assessment which are still unreleased should be scored, analyzed, and released as soon as possible.

Teachers of the Arts

The quality and success of arts education in the United States ultimately rests with those who teach the arts. It is the teachers who are responsible for fostering students' creativity and for conveying to them a sense of civilization.

The issues of teacher preparation are many and difficult. Certification requirements and staffing practices are different for general classroom teachers and specialists, and vary from state to state, between elementary and secondary schools, and among art disciplines. And, once trained, teachers, like other professionals, need opportunities to develop their abilities, to keep up with new findings in the teaching profession and in the subjects they teach. They also need administrative support and the resources to succeed.

ELEMENTARY SCHOOL CLASSROOM TEACHERS

Elementary school classroom teachers are generally expected to be able to teach all subjects (including the arts), but the pattern of their education in arts teaching varies markedly among states. Some require them to take a college course on how to teach the arts in general; some require methods courses in teaching both art and music; some require only a single course in either art or music; and some require a course from such options as drama, health or speech.

As recently as 1984, only 26 states or special jurisdictions reported having requirements for specific hours or units in the arts for certification of classroom teachers (see Figure 15). Even in jurisdictions requiring education *methods* courses in arts pedagogy, these often amount to little more than disconnected "singing" and "art-making" projects and rarely provide real substance or show how the arts can help illuminate the learning of other subjects.

Because of their lack of experience and training, many classroom teachers feel insecure in teaching the arts, especially when they are asked to include them in their basic curriculum. Providing opportunities, incentives, and funding to enable such teachers to improve and deepen their knowledge of the arts and how they should be taught is essential.

ARTS SPECIALISTS

Arts specialists are usually committed to a single arts discipline. They frequently enter teacher preparation programs as much because they want to practice their own art as because they want to educate young people in art. And, since arts teachers cannot generally guide students to levels of creation and performance beyond their own capabilities, arts teacher preparation has traditionally included a strong grounding in the practice of the arts.

Figure 15. Arts Requirements for Elementary Classroom Teacher Certification

STATE	Required Course(s)	Units Required
ALASKA	Art Methods Music Methods	1 credit 1 credit
ARIZONA	Arts	0-4 hours[1]
ARKANSAS	Public School Art Public School Music	3 hours 3 hours
DISTRICT OF COLUMBIA	Art Music	3 hours 3 hours
GEORGIA	Creative Arts[2]	5 quarter hours
HAWAII	Music Drama (Optional) Creative Arts (Optional)	4-7 hours
IDAHO	Art or Music	3 hours
INDIANA	Art or Music	3 hours
KENTUCKY	Visual Art Music	3 hours 3 hours
LOUISIANA	Elementary Arts or Music	3 hours
MARYLAND	Arts	2 credits
MASSACHUSETTS	Arts Music	3 hours 3 hours
MISSISSIPPI	Arts for Children Music Education	3 hours 3 hours
MISSOURI	Arts Education Music Education	3 hours 3 hours
NEBRASKA	Arts Methods Music Methods	3 hours 3 hours
NEW JERSEY	Creative Arts	3 hours
OHIO	Visual Arts Music	4 hours 4 hours
OREGON	Arts	2-6 quarter hours
PENNSYLVANIA	Arts Music	3 hours 3 hours
PUERTO RICO	Visual Arts Drama Music Appreciation	2 credits 2 credits 2 credits
SOUTH CAROLINA	Arts	4-6 units
SOUTH DAKOTA	Arts Methods	2 hours
TENNESSEE	Art Music	3 quarter hours 3 quarter hours
VIRGINIA	Art Music	3 hours 3 hours
WEST VIRGINIA	Art Music	2 units 2 units
WYOMING	Art, Music or Drama (Methods)	3 hours

1. Credit hours vary depending upon which of the three state universities attended.
2. For Early Childhood majors, includes visual arts, music, dance and drama.

Note: States that do not employ art and music specialists often do not require their prospective elementary classroom teachers to take courses in methods of teaching art and music.

Source: Council of Chief State School Officers, *Arts Education and the States: A Survey of State Education Policies*, Washington, D.C., September 1985, Table 4, p. 28.

The teacher accreditation standards set by the National Association of Schools of Art and Design, the National Association of Schools of Dance, the National Association of Schools of Music, and the National Association of Schools of Theatre generally recommend that prospective arts teachers take at least half of their college course work in their disciplines.

For example, degree programs accredited by the National Association of Schools of Music typically require 120-132 semester hours of college credit in music: 50 percent in basic musicianship and performance; 30-35 percent in general studies; and 15-20 percent in professional education. Prospective music teachers must acquire some competency in conducting, performing, composing, and arranging, and some mastery of keyboard, wind, string, percussion, and fretted instruments. They must also be able to transpose, improvise, and have enough vocal skill for demonstration purposes. The prospective teacher is expected to understand a range of musical styles and works, including the music of many cultures.

Undergraduate visual arts and theater teacher education programs generally offer two options: a "professional degree," which, like music, requires that 50-60 percent of the course work be in the discipline, and a "liberal arts" degree in which 35-40 percent of the course work is in the discipline and 35-40 percent in general studies.

The preparation of dance teachers presents special problems. Since most states do not have specific certification programs in dance, those who wish to teach dance must usually seek certification in another subject area, often physical education. But college physical education courses are generally irrelevant to would-be teachers of dance.

We know of no state which certifies elementary or secondary school teachers specifically in design arts, although visual arts specialists may take course work in this area. Similarly, in media arts, we know of no specific certification requirements, although film history or criticism may be included in the education of some English teachers. Some visual arts teacher training programs include courses in photography, video, and film.

Imbalance in the Training of Arts Specialists

Preparation programs for arts teachers have always emphasized skill acquisition, creation, and practice over history, critical analysis, aesthetics, and the philosophy of the arts. If arts education is to provide an understanding of the artistic heritage, as stipulated in most state curriculum guides, teacher preparation programs must provide more training in the historical/critical aspects of the arts. Future arts teachers must also be able to relate the teaching of their art to other arts, other subject areas, and the history of ideas, for the arts are an integral part of

history, philosophy, anthropology, and the other humanities disciplines.

Education of arts specialists must also place more emphasis on how the content of an art relates to how it is taught. Arts teacher preparation programs are now taught either by professors of arts education trained in the art form and in teaching methods, or by professors in departments of education (with subject matter taught by members of a university department in one of the art forms). Professors in education departments are likely to emphasize the philosophy, history, and psychology of *education*, rather than the philosophy, history and subject matter of the arts. Methods courses should be taught by professors who are expert in both education and at least one of the arts disciplines.

Finally, it is imperative that faculty members in schools of education continually test their ideas about arts teaching not only in *their* classrooms, but in elementary and secondary school classrooms. That is where their ideas will be put into practice.

State Standards and Testing for Arts Teacher Certification

Teachers are certified by state agencies to teach specific subjects and grade levels. Certification is achieved either by graduating from a state accredited university or college program or by passing either a general or subject-specific state test. State standards for these programs directly affect teacher preparation.

State credentialing agencies need to strengthen standards for arts teacher preparation programs. These are usually set at lower levels than those of either national accrediting associations or of larger colleges and universities. As a result, prospective arts teachers, especially those with bachelors' degrees, can shop around to find the least demanding program with the fewest requirements so they can move quickly into a teaching position.

States should also establish credentialing requirements in disciplines other than visual art and music. While virtually all 50 states certify art and music teachers, only 24 certify theater teachers, and only 16 certify dance teachers. (See Figure 16, pp. 106-107.) Indeed, preparation for theater and dance teacher certification is generally the province of English and physical education departments. In 1987, the Working group on the Arts in Higher Education (a cooperative project of the arts accrediting associations and the International Council of Fine Arts Deans) recommended that "changing this situation must become one of the highest priorities of the arts community in the United States." (*Teacher Education in the Arts Disciplines*, p. 13). Of equally high priority is developing credentialing requirements in the media and design arts.

Comprehensive examinations should be designed to test a prospective teacher's competency in the art of teaching the arts, in planning acceptable units of instruction, and in teaching creation, performance, history, and analysis. Current testing procedures are generally limited to multiple-choice questions relating to the history of the art form, technical information, and teaching procedures. Generally, they do little more than screen out the least competent. During 1985-86, only 14 states required prospective music teachers to pass even these tests, although 12 more have indicated that before 1989 they plan to administer tests like the National Teachers Examination in Music.

Figure 16. State Teacher Certification for Arts Specialists

STATE	Elementary						Secondary					
	Arts in General	Creative Writing	Dance	Drama	Music	Visual Art	Arts in General	Creative Writing	Dance	Drama	Music	Visual Art
Alabama	●				●	●					●	●
Alaska												
American Samoa												
Arizona					●	●	●	●	●	●	●	●
Arkansas					●	●					●	●
California							●	●	●	●	●	●
Colorado	●				●		●			●	●	
Connecticut					●	●					●	●
Delaware		●			●	●		●		●	●	●
District of Columbia					●	●					●	●
Florida	●	●	●	●	●	●	●	●	●	●	●	●
Georgia			●	●	●	●			●	●	●	●
Hawaii											●	●
Idaho					●	●				●	●	●
Illinois	●				●	●	●				●	●
Indiana	●				●	●	●				●	●
Iowa					●	●				●	●	●
Kansas				●	●	●				●	●	●
Kentucky					●	●					●	●
Louisiana					●	●					●	●
Maine	●				●		●				●	
Maryland			●	●	●	●			●	●	●	●
Massachusetts			●	●	●	●			●	●	●	●
Michigan	●		●		●	●	●		●		●	●
Minnesota					●	●					●	●
Mississippi			●		●	●			●		●	●
Missouri					●	●					●	●
Montana					●	●					●	●

STATE	Elementary						Secondary					
	Arts in General	Creative Writing	Dance	Drama	Music	Visual Art	Arts in General	Creative Writing	Dance	Drama	Music	Visual Art
Nebraska	•			•	•	•	•			•	•	•
Nevada	•				•	•	•			•	•	•
New Hampshire					•	•					•	•
New Jersey	•			•	•		•			•	•	
New Mexico					•	•				•	•	•
New York					•	•					•	•
North Carolina			•	•	•	•			•	•	•	•
North Dakota	•				•	•	•				•	•
Ohio			•		•	•			•		•	•
Oklahoma				•	•	•				•	•	•
Oregon					•	•					•	•
Pennsylvania	•	•	•	•	•	•	•	•	•	•	•	•
Puerto Rico				•	•	•				•	•	•
Rhode Island			•		•	•			•		•	•
South Carolina	•				•		•				•	
South Dakota	•				•		•				•	
Tennessee					•	•					•	•
Texas				•	•	•			•	•	•	•
Utah					•				•	•	•	•
Vermont					•	•			•		•	•
Virginia					•	•				•	•	•
Virgin Islands	•				•	•	•				•	•
Washington					•		•				•	
West Virginia					•	•					•	•
Wisconsin			•	•	•	•			•	•	•	•
Wyoming	•				•		•			•	•	
TOTAL	16	3	11	13	50	42	18	5	16	24	52	45

Many states provide K-12 certification per subject area, without distinguishing between elementary and secondary levels. For those states, a symbol appears in both elementary and secondary columns above.

Source: Council of Chief State School Officers, *Arts, Education and the States: A Survey of State Education Policies*, Washington, DC, September 1985, Table 3, pp. 26-27. Updated by the National Endowment for the Arts.

Professional Development of Arts Specialists

Teachers, like other professionals, need opportunities to grow in knowledge and expertise after certification, either during the school year or in summer. There are a number of voluntary opportunities for professional development of arts teachers, and some state education agencies and local school districts impose mandatory requirements, generally based on the acquisition of in-service credits (both through university courses and workshops and short courses offered within schools and school districts). Nonetheless, comprehensive systematic plans for helping arts teachers to develop professionally are rare.

Voluntary opportunities for professional growth include membership in professional organizations; study of professional literature; contacts with other professionals, informally and through conferences; attendance at exhibitions and performances; and travel. Teachers thus learn from other teachers and keep up with important issues in their fields. For example, visual arts teachers can learn in this way about the toxic nature of some art materials.

Unfortunately, opportunities to engage in such activities vary greatly among the different arts and among different school districts. About half the music specialists belong to the major national music educators association; only a fifth of visual arts specialists belong to theirs. Time off and funding to attend meetings and other functions are often not available, and there are few incentive programs to encourage the systematic professional development of arts teachers.

Many district art and music supervisors and curriculum coordinators, who formerly provided on-the-job help and facilitated professional contacts among arts teachers through district meetings and workshops, have been replaced by general supervisors with little or no expertise in the arts.

REFORM IN THE TEACHING PROFESSION: IMPLICATIONS FOR ARTS TEACHERS

Arts teacher preparation and professionalism will no doubt be influenced by the national debate on these subjects generally. Two major reports have recently brought national attention to the issues involved. In 1984, a consortium of education deans and chief academic officers from major universities — known as the Holmes Group — undertook a critical analysis of teacher education. Their April 1986 report, *Tomorrow's Teachers: A Report of the Holmes Group,* called for several reforms. In May 1986, the Task Force on Teaching as a Profession, a 14-member group assembled by the Carnegie Forum on Education and the Economy, also presented a report, *A Nation Prepared: Teachers for the 21st Century,* which generated suggestions for changes in the education of teachers.

The recommendations of these two reports were similar in many respects. Both concluded that:

- Teachers should be better prepared in one or more of the basic disciplines of the liberal arts or sciences, and teacher education should occur at the graduate level *after* candidates receive a broad education.

- Graduate programs in education should be based on a new professional curriculum leading to a master's degree in teaching that would include supervised practice teaching and strong relationships between schools and institutions of higher education, to advance both teaching practice and research on it.

- Increasing numbers of minority students make more urgent the need to recruit more minorities into the teaching profession.

- Career ladders and competitive salaries should be developed to allow teachers to advance in their profession and assume greater responsibilities.

- School structures and working conditions should be reformed to give teachers more authority to decide how best to meet state and local education goals, while remaining accountable for achievement of those goals.

In addition, the Carnegie report calls for a "National Board for Professional Teaching Standards." The Board would establish competency standards, assess the qualifications of those seeking certification, and grant entry-level certificates and advanced certificates to qualified applicants. Such certification would parallel the processes used by other professions, such as law or architecture.

On the positive side, if a significant number of elementary school classroom teachers were to acquire bachelors' degrees in one of the arts disciplines before entering a teacher education program, adoption of the basic principles of the Holmes Group and Carnegie report proposals would permit differentiated staffing of arts instruction in elementary schools. Such preparation would enable general classroom teachers to coordinate arts programs in elementary schools where arts specialists are not employed. It would also allow more time at the undergraduate level for specialists to study their arts disciplines in greater detail and depth.

On the negative side, sequential training in the arts disciplines before exposure to arts education methods could weaken or eliminate the parallel development of expertise in content and methodology that now characterizes some of the best undergraduate arts education programs. In these exemplary programs, future arts teachers observe arts teaching in schools during their freshman and sophomore years in college and serve as teacher apprentices in their junior and senior years. Arts education methodology courses are interrelated with arts courses and taught by professors of arts education rather than by general education specialists.

SPECIALIST OR CLASSROOM TEACHER: WHO SHOULD TEACH THE ARTS IN ELEMENTARY SCHOOL?

The debate as to whether elementary school classroom teachers are adequately prepared to teach the arts, which began at the turn of the century, continues today without resolution. The addition to the curriculum of dance, design, media, theater, and creative writing makes the question even more complicated.

Those who argue for arts specialists in elementary schools emphasize the specialist's knowledge of the arts and experience in teaching the arts, particularly creation and performance. Many arts specialists insist that a teacher who does not know how to play a musical instrument, read music, write a poem, draw the human figure in action, dance, or act — cannot possibly teach children anything substantive about these arts.

Those who argue for classroom teachers teaching the arts in elementary schools note that, as pointed out below, there is a scarcity of arts specialists. Moreover, they say, elementary school classroom teachers are no more unprepared to teach the arts than they are to teach science or history. They argue that staffing elementary schools with arts specialists makes the arts specialized as opposed to a basic part of the curriculum, working against the kind of individual nurturing that comes from prolonged experience with one teacher and preventing the teacher from interweaving the arts with other subjects. Further, the classroom teacher may be better able to use time flexibly and in fact spend more time on the arts, while specialists must adhere to strict schedules, such as one 40-50 minute period per week, or 30 hours a year.

The Endowment takes the view that excellent elementary school arts instruction depends less on specialists than it does on integration of specialist and classroom teacher instruction. The specialist provides a depth of instruction beyond the capability of most classroom teachers, while the classroom teacher relates the arts to other subject areas and uses classroom time flexibly to accommodate both long and short periods of arts instruction according to the requirements of the projects and of the school day. Nonetheless, as we have said, it remains essential to upgrade the arts education of general classroom teachers. The pilot project of the Getty Center for Education in the Arts, which helps classroom teachers to teach the visual arts, is an important contribution in this area.

THE SCARCITY OF ARTS SPECIALISTS

According to the 1987 U.S. Department of Education survey of school districts (1987 district survey), nearly half of elementary schools have no visual arts specialists, and 16 percent of them have no music specialists. Although the survey did not collect data on specialists in other arts fields, it seems likely that if dance, drama, design, literature, the media, and creative writing are taught at all in elementary schools, they are taught by classroom teachers. The 1987 district survey also showed that shortages of arts specialists are several times greater than shortages of English and social studies teachers, exceeded only by shortages of foreign language specialists.

On the other hand, according to a 1983 study of the National

Figure 17. Percentage of School Districts Indicating They Had a Shortage, Balance, or Surplus of Teachers in Selected Fields, 1986-87 (50 States and D.C.)

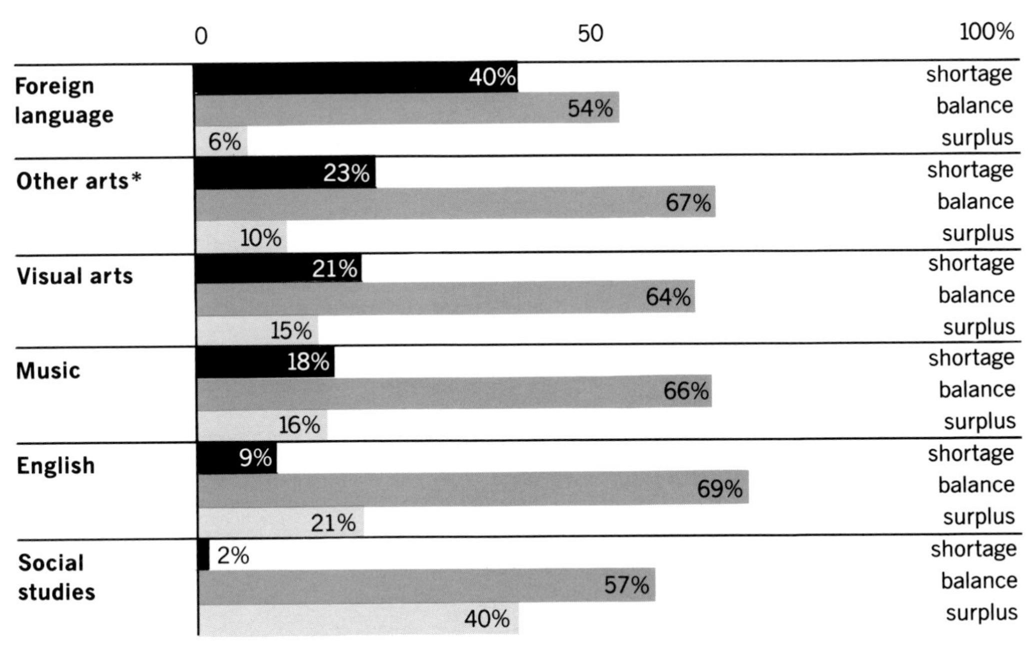

*Includes dance, drama, and creative writing.

This information is based on the opinions or perceptions of knowledgeable district personnel, rather than precise data obtained from records of applications.

Source: Center for Education Statistics, "Public School District Policies and Practices in Selected Aspects of Arts and Humanities Instruction," U.S. Department of Education Bulletin, February 1988, Figure 6, p. 11.

Figure 18. Teachers and Teacher Candidate Shortages*, November 1983, in Public and Private Elementary and Secondary Schools (50 states and D.C., data in full-time equivalents)

No. Teachers	No. Candidate Shortages	SUBJECT and Number of FTE Shortages*/1000 Teachers
29,900	263	Bilingual Education 8.8
264,100	1,027	Special Education 3.9
9,200	34	Computer Sciences 3.7
50,700	184	Art 3.6
79,100	243	Music 3.1
43,700	82	Industrial Arts 1.9
147,100	263	Mathematics 1.8
131,100	225	Biological & Physical Sciences 1.7
50,400	77	Foreign Languages 1.5
64,300	68	Vocational Education 1.1
182,700	171	English Language Arts .9
873,300	742	General Elementary Education .8
142,400	67	Social Studies/Social Sciences .5
485,300	519	Other Teachers 1.1
2,553,300	3,965	TOTAL TEACHERS 1.6

(Bar chart scale: 0 1 2 3 4 5 6 7 8 9 10)

*Shortages defined as "positions vacant, abolished, or transferred to another field because a candidate was unable to be found."

Source: Center for Education Statistics, "Teachers in Elementary and Secondary Education," U.S. Department of Education, March 1987, Table 7, pp. 4 and 13.

Center for Educational Statistics, there are almost as many art and music teachers in the schools as there are science teachers. (See Figure 18, p. 112.) Teacher candidate shortages in art and music are small (notwithstanding that they are higher than in any other subject except bilingual education, special education, and computer education).

Today's shortage of arts teacher candidates can be expected to become more acute in the next five years, consistent with projections in the teaching profession generally. In *A Nation Prepared* (1986), the Carnegie Task Force on Teaching as a Profession reported that with the end of the "baby boom" in the 1970's, few new teachers were hired and some teachers, usually those with the least seniority, were dismissed. The average age of teachers rose as a consequence, and many are now near retirement, so that many school districts face a situation in which half their teachers may have to be replaced within the next three or four years.

The Task Force went on to report that as the children of the "baby boom" enter school we can anticipate a steep increase in the annual demand for teachers — from 115,000 in 1981 to 215,000 in 1992. But arts teacher preparation programs have diminished in size since the 1970's and may not be able adequately to serve large numbers of new candidates.

RECOMMENDATIONS

1. **Teacher Preparation and Certification.** State certifying agencies should strengthen arts certification requirements for all teachers whose responsibilities include the arts. Training of all teachers — elementary school classroom teachers, specialist arts teachers, and teachers of other subjects to which the arts are relevant — should include (i) study of important works of art (their craft, history, and significance to the civilizations which they symbolize) and (ii) study of techniques for creating or performing one of the arts. To this end:

A. *For elementary school classroom teachers,* each state certifying agency should establish arts requirements for certification; over half of the states do not have such requirements. These requirements should include at least two courses in the arts which stress content.

B. *For K-12 arts specialists,* each state certifying agency should require training in the history and critical analysis of the art form, as well as in production and performance. Half the university course work should be in the art discipline, and methods courses in arts education should be made an integral part of substantive instruction in the arts, not separated out as recommended in the Holmes and Carnegie reports. University courses in the arts disciplines should, where relevant, draw on the standards and recommendations of the National Association of Schools of Art and Design, the National Association of Schools of Music, the National Association of Schools of Theatre, and the National Association of Schools of Dance. Faculty responsible for teaching these courses should test their ideas about arts teaching in actual teaching situations in elementary and secondary classrooms.

C. Teacher recruitment and certification in the arts of dance, design, the media, and theater should be strengthened and instituted in those states which do not now provide for them.

D. In a time when we are likely to face a shortage of qualified arts teachers, state certifying agencies should develop and implement flexible procedures that provide for special testing and certification of experienced practicing artists and arts professionals who can demonstrate a comprehensive background in the arts and substantial knowledge of the issues and methodology of K-12 arts education.

E. *For teachers of other subjects (such as history, geography, and foreign languages),* state certifying agencies and colleges and universities should require a basic general education in the arts. The arts are related to all school subjects, and all teachers should understand them well enough to use them to support and elucidate instruction in other subjects and to show how such subjects can contribute to an understanding of the arts.

F. Testing of teacher qualifications should be mandated as a condition of teacher certification. State certifying agencies should develop tests to evaluate teacher preparation and teacher preparation programs. Such tests should assess the general (liberal arts) preparation of teachers, their knowledge of art in the context of history and culture, their ability to analyze art, their performance and skill competencies, their knowledge of issues in arts education, and their skill in lesson planning and pedagogy.

G. Teacher preparation programs should emphasize the importance of working with local artists and arts institutions and provide information on how to draw on them.

2. **Teacher Recruitment.** Arts education professional associations, state departments of education, colleges and universities, and arts schools should undertake efforts to attract capable students to arts teacher preparation programs, including minority students. Special efforts should be made to recruit dance, design, media, and drama teachers.

3. **Teacher Professional Development.** Arts teachers, no less than teachers of other subjects, should be provided with opportunities to advance within their profession. State education agencies and school districts should develop standards and incentives to this end, and should promote career mobility within the school, district, region, or state. Such incentives should include full or partial reimbursement of expenses for summer studies and for attending professional meetings and conferences.

4. **Teaching Environment.** Local school districts should, consistent with state and local mandates, provide arts teachers with maximum flexibility to meet the individual needs of specific classes. They should also provide arts teachers with adequate compensation, facilities, administrative support, and teaching materials.

5. **Optimum Staffing.** Each school district should aim to provide arts instruction by trained arts specialists at all levels K-12. To this end:
   A. Elementary school administrators should recruit teacher curriculum coordinators for each of the arts. Where available, arts specialists should be given this responsibility; where they are not available, classroom teachers with particular interests and qualifications in the arts should serve as coordinators in the interim. Coordinators should be given time and resources and be responsible for developing sequential arts programming, for assembling necessary resources, and for assisting teachers. Professional arts education associations, artists, and arts organizations can help the coordinators in these efforts.

   B. Elementary school administrators should, especially in the upper elementary grades, assign the best arts teachers to teach the arts in several classrooms in addition to their own. In such a program, students would benefit from competent instruction and the number of subjects for which teachers would have to prepare would be reduced.

   C. In middle, junior high, and high schools, all arts classes should continue to be taught by arts specialists, or if no arts specialist is available, by qualified people in the community, including experienced artists or arts professionals.

Michelangelo, *Creation of Adam*, Sistine Chapel, Rome, Alinari/Art Resource, New York

Research Priorities in Arts Education

As we seek to improve the way in which the arts are taught, it is imperative that a solid foundation of research information be available to guide our actions. Research in arts education should focus on matters that can actually improve what is done in the classroom and include:

1. surveys and critical analyses of the goals, purposes, and curricular content of arts education;

2. analyses of arts education program requirements including time, personnel, resource materials, and organizational and administrative support systems;

3. historical inquiries;

4. studies of learner development, behavior, perception, attitude, and knowledge;

5. studies of teaching methodologies;

6. studies of the effects of experimental and ongoing arts education programs; and

7. analyses of how research findings can affect study of the arts in the classroom.

THE LONELY TASK OF THE RESEARCHER IN ARTS EDUCATION

Most arts education research is conducted by college and university professors, and only a very small percentage of these work consistently and full-time as researchers. Since many arts education professors' first commitment is to the art form as artists, they tend to allocate most of their time and energy to that and to teaching. Research takes last place in the professional lives of most arts educators.

The small number of professors who make a priority of arts education research find that it requires an enormous personal commitment of time and money since there are no steady and dependable sources of funding. In other disciplines, academic researchers have greater access to outside support, and department heads can arrange lighter teaching assignments for them by hiring instructors to take over their courses. Arts education researchers, on the other hand, must usually conduct their research without such help, while meeting the obligations of a full academic schedule and of their own artistic careers. It is a wonder that we have the small but growing body of arts education research that we do.

VARIETIES OF RESEARCH

There are several kinds of arts education research. The first, which regularly appears in the journals, is quantitative, usually involving the isolation and manipulation of discrete variables and the methodologies of behavioral and cognitive psychology. This kind of research deals with such matters as the effect of speed alternations on tempo note selection, the effects of exposure to classical music on the musical preferences of preschool children, the effects of listening instructions and cognitive style on music appreciation, and the effect of verbal contextual information in processing visual art. These quantitative studies need to be interpreted if they are to provide information that can be actually used by teachers and administrators to improve the curriculum and instruction.

A second type of research, which appears less often in the journals, involves looking at the arts classroom as a whole. This research relates to qualitative sociological and anthropological inquiry, and even to arts criticism. It is voluminous and difficult to condense for publication in research journals or to summarize for practitioners.

A third, hybrid form of research is beginning to emerge which combines both quantitative and qualitative methods. The J. Paul Getty Trust's Center for Arts Education recently commissioned a set of studies of this kind of the visual arts programs of seven school districts, describing them in qualitative terms and reporting their outcomes in terms of test scores and other measures.

The question of how best to conduct research in arts education is still very much a matter of debate. Those who favor quantitative experimental research fault the qualitative researchers for being too impressionistic, while those favoring qualitative inquiry fault the quantitative researchers for seeing only the trees and missing the forest. What seems less a matter for debate, however, is the fact that arts education researchers, whatever methods they follow, are severely limited by factors of both time and financial support.

It is also clear that the existing research in music and art needs to be supplemented, and that a variety of research needs to be undertaken in dance, theater, design, media, and creative writing education.

Existing Research in the Field

Arts education researchers are distributed unevenly across the disciplines. There has been very little research in dance, creative writing, and theater education — and practically none in design and media education. It is worth noting, however, that research in theater education is increasing and the *Youth Theatre Journal,* which used to devote one issue a year to research, now includes theater education research in each issue. Music is probably the only area in which there is a sufficient body of empirical research to permit researchers to build their work on the findings of earlier studies.

The federally sponsored Educational Research Information Center (ERIC) regularly publishes abstracts of research on education, including arts education. Over 3,000 documents in ERIC relating to arts education were reviewed for this report. This collection of abstracts of articles and other writings includes 1,073 articles on arts education in general, 1,371 on literature and creative writing, 1,647 on the visual arts, 982 on music, 443 on theater, 246 on dance, and 223 on film. Many of the articles cover two or more fields.

Figure 19. The Contents of Arts Literature in the Educational Resources Information Center (ERIC) (1966-86)

	NUMBER	Case For	Goals	Programs	Curricula	Teaching Guides/Instrnl. Materials	Resources	Testing	Attitudes	Evaluation of Ed. Programs	Special Populations	Psych. of Learning
		PERCENT*										
Arts General	1073	29	11	11	5	16	9	2	1	4	8	5
Music	982	11	7	11	4	31	12	4	3	4	16	13
Visual Arts	1647	6	4	13	9	38	4	2	1	6	8	9
Theater	443	6	18	8	13	32	16	3	2	5	14	7
Dance	246	7	22	9	20	33	2	1	2	5	2	2
Lit/Creative Writing	1371	7	8	4	6	36	17	4	5	5	8	2
Film	223	—	13	8	21	35	18	4	3	6	1	6
TOTAL	5985**											

*Percentages may total more than 100, because some documents were classified in more than one category.
**Duplicated entries.

Source: "Analysis of ERIC System Abstracts on Arts Education," prepared for the National Endowment for the Arts by Child Trends, Inc., June 1987.

Two observations are necessary. First, the ERIC arts education system is incomplete in that numerous articles from major arts education journals (e.g., *Journal of Aesthetic Education, Research in Visual Arts Education,* and *Design for Arts in Education)* are not included. Second, the majority of the articles discuss goals, justifications, and descriptions of arts education programs, rather than their actual results.

Nevertheless, the ERIC collection provides a profile of the concerns of arts educators and demonstrates the omissions, strengths, and weaknesses of arts education research. Eighty-one percent of the general arts education articles were written primarily to advocate specific views, while only 7 percent contained substantive research and evaluation. This balance was evident in the discipline specific articles as well:

	Description & Advocacy	Research & Evaluation
Dance	93%	8%
Literature	78%	14%
Music	76%	11%
Theater	93%	10%
Visual Arts	74%	9%

Note: Percentages may add up to more than 100 due to double-counting.

The *Journal of Research in Music Education,* now in its 35th year of publication by the Music Educators National Conference, and *Studies in Art Education,* now in its 25th year of publication by the National Art Education Association, represent the highest standards of research in arts education. The music education research articles are mostly concerned with learner and program outcomes. The visual arts research articles, on the other hand, are mostly concerned with the nature of arts education and critical analyses of the contents of art curricula. About a fifth of the music education articles and about a tenth of the visual arts articles relate to the history of their respective arts.

These research differences reflect the fact that the content and goals of music education are stable, while those of visual arts education are still subjects of extensive debate. A major shift in the perceived goals for teaching the visual arts in school has occurred since the 1950's and 1960's when it was thought that visual arts teaching should aim primarily at stimulating personal expression and creativity. The 1980's perception is that visual arts teaching should not only instruct students in studio methods, but also provide a sense of civilization through the study of art history, criticism, and aesthetics. Although this shift has been reflected in the articles in *Studies in Art Education,* there is little substantial research on this approach in terms of student achievement.

An important exception to the general lack of arts education research is Project Zero at Harvard University. Founded in 1967, Project Zero has since the early 1970's conducted wide-ranging research on artistic development, thinking, and learning. In recent years, Project Zero researchers have begun to direct some of their efforts to the problems of arts education. In collaboration with researchers at the Educational Testing Service, Project Zero is now working with school systems to develop instructional tools and research and assessment methodologies. (See Chapter 4, "The Case for Testing and Evaluation in the Arts.")

FEDERAL HELP FOR ARTS EDUCATION RESEARCH

From 1965 to 1970, the U.S. Office of Education underwrote a large number of research projects in the arts and supported a number of conferences, seminars, and symposia with arts education research on the agenda. However, since that time and until recently, no agency of the federal government has provided continuing support of comprehensive research in arts education.

In 1986, however, the U.S. Department of Education approached the National Endowment for the Arts with a view to establishing centers for arts and literature education research, as a part of an overall research effort in elementary and secondary education. Centers for the fields of science, mathematics, and elementary subjects (including the arts) have now been established to explore what students learn, how they are taught and how student learning is assessed. The Department of Education is planning a five-year funding of the Elementary Subjects Center, which, among other things, will provide useful information about arts education at the elementary school level.

In September 1987, the U.S. Department of Education and the National Endowment for the Arts established an arts education research center with two divisions; three-year funding for this effort is planned. One division is based at New York University, and the other at the University of Illinois at Champaign-Urbana. Initial findings of the center will be forthcoming in the fall of 1988. In addition, the U.S. Department of Education, also in cooperation with the Endowment, established in November 1987 a research center in the learning and teaching of literature at the State University of New York at Albany.

The University of Illinois will conduct a number of specific research studies including: status surveys of arts education in the visual arts, music, dance, and theater; cultural literacy in the visual arts; achievement testing in visual art; motivation in music; music in general

Basket, Shoshonean, Fernandinos Mission, California, before 1920, Smithsonian Institution, Department of Anthropology, Cat. #64687, Washington

education; cultural factors affecting visual arts learning; development of a K-12 dance curriculum with a pilot program at the elementary level; construction of a theater curriculum for K-12 district-wide programs; and observational case studies on evaluating arts learning in the classroom. The goal is to learn from these studies ways and means to further arts instruction in the nation's schools.

At New York University's School of Education, Health, Nursing, and Arts Professions (SEHNAP) in New York City, the center will take a less traditional research approach focused directly on the teaching of art and music in junior and senior high schools. Initially, 10 oustanding teachers in five New York City schools will analyze the curriculum and student learning in their classrooms. Through this process, teachers will master research skills which they will use in their own classrooms to improve arts instruction. They, along with the University researchers, will work with a second group of 20 teachers nationally to validate the exemplary teaching techniques identified in the first year.

This collaboration in research centers involves planning for Department of Education funding of just over $4.6 million (including funding of an Elementary Subjects Center which includes the arts) and National Endowment for the Arts funding of approximately $1.5 million over three to five years.

This collaboration followed two other joint research projects between the Department of Education and the Arts Endowment. In 1984, the two agencies joined with the Rockefeller Foundation in supporting a survey of state policies and resources in the area of arts education, undertaken by the Council of Chief State School Officers. And, in early 1987, the two agencies collaborated with the Humanities Endowment in funding a survey of district-level policies and resources in the area of arts and humanities education (see "Leadership in Arts Education," pp. 142-144).

RECOMMENDATIONS

More sustained support is needed to improve research in arts education. Such support should help attract better graduate students, assist apprenticeships, and permit the best researchers to undertake significant long-term studies on arts education. Research priorities should be thoughtfully established by funders in consultation with arts educators in order (i) to improve classroom instruction and (ii) to achieve a balance between the interests of individual researchers and general research needs. To this end:

A. National, state, and local funders (public and private) should increase their priority for arts education research.

B. The U. S. Department of Education and the National Endowment for the Arts should explore ways to assure that educational statistics, surveys, and reports cover the arts with the same attention and detail as for other school subjects. One of the Educational Resource Information Centers (ERIC) should enter into the system the large backlog of documents from previously published arts education research and periodically survey current sources of information to be entered into the system in the future.

C. Reports should be generated to synthesize and disseminate the results of completed studies, to make them available to classroom teachers and serve as bases for further research.

D. Comprehensive baseline data should be collected and periodically updated to establish trend lines concerning the extent to which education programs in each of the arts are in fact established in states and school districts. These should include data on curricula and course offerings, teachers, student enrollment, materials, facilities, classroom time, budgets, administrative support, testing and evaluation techniques, and learning outcomes.

E. Research is needed to learn what kinds of teacher training, curriculum development, instructional methodology, and resources are most effective in improving arts education.

F. Research is needed to tell us what can and should be taught at what ages and how it can best be taught. Research should be included on the complete act of learning—students' interactions with teachers, the use of resources in specific classrooms, and the influence of the family and environment on learning in the arts in comparison to learning in other subjects. Research is needed to provide more information on how students acquire knowledge of, and learn to interpret, the arts; how students perceive, value, perform, create, and use the arts; and how learning in the arts broadens perspective, gives a sense of the human condition, and fosters reasoning ability.

Leadership in Arts Education

What is taught in America's schools reflects the values of American society, the ideals of the nation, the educational goals of the states, and the demands of local communities.

Shortcomings in American education are a recognized matter of national concern. When the 1984 National Assessment of Educational Progress reports that 12 percent of eighth-grade students say they do no writing in school and 40 percent of 13-year-olds do not have even intermediate-level reading skills, state legislatures, state departments of education, and school administrators take action.

Statistics on arts education may cause less alarm: most Americans will not likely consider the nation at risk because less than half of 17-year-old high school students could identify Rembrandt's *Night Watch* as the significant work in comparison to three ordinary works. But concern for "cultural literacy" appears to be on the rise. E. D. Hirsch's *Cultural Literacy* and Alan Bloom's *The Closing of the American Mind* remained on the *New York Times* nonfiction best seller list for many months, and the report of the National Endowment for the Humanities, *American Memory: A Report on the Humanities in the Nation's Public Schools,* received extensive media coverage.

Americans' concern for "cultural literacy" is understandable. Without it young Americans will lack an understanding of their society and civilization, of themselves, their nation, and the multiplicity of cultures that define what it is to be an American. This is especially important now when our young people spend something like six hours a day in front of the television screen, soaking up popular culture with little or no guidance as to how to discriminate between the good and the bad, the benevolent and malevolent.

Arts education also has practical importance. Understanding the cultures of other countries helps American business succeed in world markets, and acts as a stimulus to the creativity and problem solving which are essential to competitiveness.

Literacy in the arts is a compulsory prerequisite of "cultural literacy." But it cannot be acquired without study and hard work. If we are to have culturally literate young people, arts education, like other education, must be sequential and part of the curriculum. This can only be accomplished by popular demand which, in turn, requires strong leadership.

There are four major sectors that can help advance the cause of arts education:

1) The **governance sector** includes the President and the Congress of the United States; state governors and legislatures; mayors, county executives, and city and county councils; parents and the voters. This sector determines the societal goals to be achieved by education and allocates public monies to these ends.

2) The **education sector** includes teachers, school administrators, local boards of education, state education agencies, the U.S. Department of Education, teacher training institutions, teacher credentialing agencies, and professional associations which support education and education professionals. This sector operates and directly influences the schools; it implements education programs designed to achieve the societal goals set by the governance sector.

3) The **arts sector** includes artists and arts professionals, arts institutions, arts patrons, alliances of arts supporters, and government arts agencies at local, state, and federal levels (including the National Endowment for the Arts). This sector includes both commercial and nonprofit ventures that create, produce, present, exhibit, perform, publish, and preserve art. It also includes the film, television, recording, and publishing media.

4) The **business-producer sector** includes publishers, manufacturers, and suppliers (including audio-visual producers) of materials for use in schools. This sector produces and distributes curriculum resources and materials.

Individuals and organizations in each of the four sectors need to reach beyond their special, although sometimes overlapping interests and work together if arts education is to advance. Understanding of the four sectors and of recent examples of successful commitment to arts education can help point the way.

THE GOVERNANCE SECTOR

The arts will become part of the school curriculum only when concerned citizens work to make it happen. They are the parents and voters who elect the officials and legislators who set educational goals and establish education budgets. Citizens concerned with making arts education a basic and sequential part of the curriculum can join groups such as parent-teacher associations and student organizations, attend school board meetings, and lobby school administrators and teachers.

They must insist on basic and sequential arts education for their children.

Arts education has high standing in the governance sector. In 1985, President Reagan observed that "we must teach our children more than just hard facts and floppy disks. We must teach them the rich artistic inheritance of our culture." More recently, in June 1987, he commented: "The arts and the humanities teach us who we are and what we can be. They lie at the very core of the culture of which we're a part, and they provide the foundation from which we may reach out to other cultures so that the great heritage that is ours may be enriched by — as well as itself enrich — other enduring traditions." After quoting John Adams to the effect that his grandchildren should have "a right to study painting, poetry, music, architecture," the President stated we should "resolve that our schools will teach our children the same respect and appreciation for the arts and humanities that the Founders had."

President Reagan's views of the importance of the arts and of arts education in American life have been shared by Presidents from George Washington on.

The Congress is also on record in supporting the importance of arts education. In 1985, it called for this report, and also amended the Endowment's enabling legislation to include in the Congressional Declaration of Purpose for the two National Endowments the following finding: "Americans should receive in school background and preparation in the arts and humanities to enable them to recognize and appreciate the aesthetic dimensions of our lives, the diversity of excellence that comprises our cultural heritage, and artistic and scholarly expression."

Legislatures at the state level are similarly on record. In 1983, the National Conference of State Legislatures adopted the following policy resolution: "The performing, visual, and literary arts are an essential element of the quality of life in every state, a means of creative expression, and a source of enjoyment for all. The opportunity to experience the arts should be available to every individual. The National Conference of State Legislatures encourages state legislatures to pursue policies which: Encourage the improvement of arts education programs for students and teachers, and the integration of the arts into the education curriculum."

Support of arts education comes from other parts of the governance sector. The National Congress of Parents and Teachers (the National PTA) has published articles and brochures to help local parent-teacher associations advance learning in the arts. "The National PTA believes that the arts are central to learning, and that the integration of the arts in general education is a goal of the highest

PRESIDENTIAL QUOTATIONS

George Washington
Letter to Reverend
Joseph Willard,
March 22, 1781

"The arts and sciences essential to the prosperity of the state and to the ornament and happiness of human life have a primary claim to the encouragement of every lover of his country and mankind."

John Adams
Letter to Abigail Adams
May 12, 1780

"I must study politics and war that my sons may have liberty to study mathematics and philosophy. My sons ought to study mathematics and philosophy, geography, natural history and naval architecture, navigation, commerce, and agriculture, in order to give their children a right to study painting, poetry, music, architecture. . . ."

Thomas Jefferson
Letter to James Madison,
September 20, 1785

"You see I am an enthusiast on the subject of the arts. But it is an enthusiasm of which I am not ashamed, as its object is to improve the taste of my countrymen, to increase their reputation, to reconcile to them the respect of the world, and procure them its praise."

Franklin D. Roosevelt
Address at Temple University,
Philadelphia, PA
February 22, 1936

"Inequality may linger in the world of material things, but great music, great literature, great art and the wonders of science are, and should be, open to all."

Dwight D. Eisenhower
Remarks at opening of new
American galleries at the
Metropolitan Museum of Art,
October 24, 1957

"Art is a universal language and through it each nation makes its own unique contribution to the culture of mankind."

John F. Kennedy
Remarks on behalf of the
National Cultural Center
National Guard Armory
November 29, 1962

"Art and the encouragement of art is political in the most profound sense, not as a weapon in the struggle, but as an instrument of understanding of the futility of struggle between those who share man's faith. Aeschylus and Plato are remembered today long after the triumphs of imperial Athens are gone. Dante outlived the ambitions of 13th-century Florence. Goethe stands serenely above the politics of Germany, and I am certain that after the dust of centuries has passed over our cities, we too will be remembered not for victories or defeats in battle or politics, but for our contribution to the human spirit. . . ."

Lyndon B. Johnson
Remarks at signing of the Arts and Humanities Bill, September 29, 1965

"Art is a nation's most precious heritage. For it is in our works of art that we reveal to ourselves, and to others, the inner vision which guides us as a Nation. And where there is no vision, the people perish."

Richard M. Nixon
Address at the Annual Conference of the Associated Councils of the Arts, May 26, 1971

"We, this Nation of ours, could be the richest nation in the world. We could be the most powerful nation in the world. We could be the freest nation in the world—but only if the arts are alive and flourishing can we experience the true meaning of our freedom, and know the full glory of the human spirit."

Gerald R. Ford
Message to the Congress, transmitting Annual Report of the National Endowment for the Arts and the National Council on the Arts June 23, 1976

"Our Nation has a diverse and extremely rich cultural heritage. It is a source of pride and strength to millions of Americans who look to the arts for inspiration, communication and the opportunity for creative self-expression."

Jimmy Carter
Remarks at a White House Reception National Conference of Artists April 2, 1980

"The relationship between government and art must necessarily be a delicate one. It would not be appropriate for the government to try to define what is good or what is true or what is beautiful. But government can provide nourishment to the ground within which these ideas spring forth from the seeds of inspiration within the human mind. . . ."

Ronald Reagan
Remarks at the National Medal of Arts White House Luncheon, June 18, 1987

"Why do we, as a free people, honor the arts? Well, the answer is both simple and profound. The arts and the humanities teach us who we are and what we can be. They lie at the very core of the culture of which we're a part, and they provide the foundation from which we may reach out to other cultures so that the great heritage that is ours may be enriched by — as well as itself enrich — other enduring traditions."

priority. The teaching and study of the arts in the elementary, secondary, and continuing education curriculum is a key to the complete intellectual and philosophical development of students."

Private foundations are also actively working for improved arts education. The Rockefeller Foundation played a leading role in supporting The Arts, Education and Americans Panel which in 1977 published *Coming to Our Senses.* The Carnegie Foundation for the Advancement of Teaching provided leadership in its 1983 report, *High School: A Report on Secondary Education in America* which affirmed the place of the arts as a basic subject in the high school curriculum. The J. Paul Getty Trust has made arts education one of its four major areas of funding and concern.

This rhetoric and activity is being translated into action. Since 1979, 27 states have added arts requirements for high school graduation; only two had such requirements before. Similarly, the U.S. Department of Education 1987 survey of school districts (1987 district survey) reports that a growing number of districts now require units in the arts for graduation from high school. The number reporting increases between 1982 and 1987 in the number of arts courses being offered is greater than those reporting decreases. Fifty percent of school districts report that the percentage of their budgets allocated to arts education increased during these years. While a majority of districts reported that between 1982 and 1987 the percent of classroom time in the school day for arts education stayed the same, more than a third reported that the amount of time had increased; only 6 percent reported decreases. And, state appropriations for artist residency programs have increased 71 percent in the three-year period 1983-86.

It is noteworthy that in the states most highly involved in education reform — New Jersey, North Carolina, Tennessee, Texas, and Utah, to name just five — the process has been pushed by governors and state legislators. Arts education reform in these states is treated as seriously as reform in other educational subjects. Achieving parity for arts education reform took vigilance on the part of teachers and initiative by state education leaders.

Tennessee: Working the Arts into Education Reform

In early drafts of what became the 1984 Tennessee Education Reform Act, the arts were not included. An English teacher in Eastern Tennessee, who was then Chairperson of the Tennessee Arts Commission, reported the omission to her state senator, who pointed it out to both the drafters of the educational plan and the Governor. The Governor, in cooperation with a coalition of legislators from both political parties, used the power of his office to make the arts part of what came to be called the "Better Schools Program." The political negotiations to develop the Better Schools Program included an agreement between the senator from Eastern Tennessee and the Governor that at least $1 million in new educational funds would be specifically earmarked for arts education.

As the Better Schools Program moved forward, higher amounts were allotted to the arts, a new state director of arts education was hired to develop a comprehensive plan for arts education, and three music and three visual arts consultants were brought to Tennessee to help implement it. By the 1989-90 school year, each school district in the state is required to show how its arts programs correspond to the state curriculum framework.

Tennessee also established a week-long "Tennessee Arts Academy," in which art and music teachers and classroom teachers work with six nationally recognized clinicians, lecturers, and arts specialists from across the country. In 1987 alone, approximately 15 percent of the visual arts teachers in the state had the opportunity to study at the Academy. The teachers give their time and receive in-service and college credit; other costs are borne by the state.

The Tennessee Better Schools Program also plans to place art, music, and physical education teachers in each elementary school in the state, at an estimated total cost of $44 million a year, to be phased in over a four-year period. The first phase was put into effect during the 1986-87 school year.

New Jersey: A New Emphasis on Arts Education

Another outstanding initiative is represented by New Jersey's Literacy in the Arts Act, signed into law in June 1987. This comprehensive bill resulted from the strong leadership provided by Governor Thomas H. Kean. With funding from the New Jersey State Department of Education, the bill created a task force made up of two members of the New Jersey Council on the Arts, the Chancellor of Higher Education, the President of the New Jersey State School Board Association, and the President of the State Education Association, plus 16 public members appoined by the governor.

The task force is charged with the following tasks: (1) to develop a plan to provide sequential K-12 instruction in the performing and visual arts for all young people in the state; (2) to survey all ongoing arts programs in the state and make the findings available to all school districts; (3) to evaluate the effects of arts exposure on the total educational and psychological development of students; (4) to explore the feasibility of establishing competency requirements for high school students in any of, but not limited to, the disciplines of writing, architecture, dance, and drama; and (5) to examine procedures through which teachers of visual and performing arts can obtain certification in their fields and recommend possible reforms where appropriate.

THE EDUCATION SECTOR

The most powerful force in education is the individual school, along with its principal, its teachers, and the parents who support it. The school district, with its power to shape policy and make budget allocations, is a close second. As the distance between students and teachers and decision-making authorities increases, however, real influence generally decreases. Federal or national entities, such as the U.S. Department of Education and national education membership organizations, have less influence on schools than state-level authorities and membership organizations, and these in turn are less influential than local schools and school boards.

Those outside the education sector need to mesh their efforts with state and locally mandated school programs. The arts can only become part of the basic curriculum if the education sector perceives such change to be its responsibility and interest. Giving priority to arts education requires making time in the school day, hiring qualified teachers, and producing curriculum materials. Only the education sector can do this.

For too long, however, the arts educators have shouldered most of the task of justifying and implementing arts education. While they have the expertise, they lack the clout to make the arts an educational priority. Arts education programs are seldom *expected* to be as good as they might be. Those in the education sector must reach out and join forces with members of the governance and arts sectors to advance arts education in the schools.

Leadership at the School Level

According to research known as effective schools research (summarized and analyzed by Educational Research Service, Inc.), leadership by principals is the key to higher quality school programs. Comparisons of achievements of students with similar social and economic backgrounds also show that higher quality school programs contribute to student learning. While this finding might appear to be self-evident, the research in fact rebuts James Coleman's 1966 *Equality of Educational Opportunity Study* which suggested that schools had little effect on student achievement and that socially and economically advantaged students were bound to succeed in school while socially and economically disadvantaged students were bound not to. It is important for the future of arts education programs that arts education be among the criteria for judging school "effectiveness." Today it is not.

Effective schools research identifies five major characteristics in schools where student achievement is high: strong instructional leadership, an orderly school climate, high expectations, frequent assessment of student progress, and an emphasis on basic skills. Three of these factors have particular application to arts education: strong administrative leadership, high expectations, and frequent assessment of student progress.

Administrative Leadership: According to the Phi Delta Kappa study of exceptional urban schools (1980), the leadership authority of school administrators is crucial to an "effective school." Without it, efforts by parents and others outside the schools often fail, because they lack "permanence, power, and legitimacy" (Educational Research Service, Inc., 1983, p. 26). This finding is particularly important to arts education. Most reform efforts in this area have been initiated from outside the school structure, by parents and individuals and organizations in the arts sector. Relatively few of these have been effective. An excellent example of working within the school structure is the checklist for elementary school principals developed by the National Art Education Association. (See following box.)

High Expectations: It is critical that school principals insist on programs in the arts that are as rigorous and systematic as those in reading and mathematics. As in these subjects, principals should know the arts curriculum, make frequent inquiries about the arts programs, and visit arts classrooms to observe instruction and discuss it with their teachers. If school principals expect little of arts programs other than student performances and exhibitions that reflect favorably upon the school, the programs will never be as good as they should and can be.

Frequent Assessment of Student Progress: School-wide systems for careful and frequent evaluation of student progress are also characteristic of effective schools. Such systems must be applied to arts education so that the teachers will understand that student progess in the arts is of concern to the whole school. Teachers and principals need to know what the students are actually learning so they can evaluate the effectiveness of arts instruction and offer special attention to those who need it. Progress in the arts should be of as much concern as in any other subject.

A Checklist Developed for ELEMENTARY PRINCIPALS by the National Art Education Association

SCHOOL LEADERSHIP: As the instructional leader, do you understand the value of art education to the development of a child? Does your faculty realize that your commitment to quality education includes art education? Do you work directly with the district-wide art supervisor, director, coordinator, or chairperson to ensure a quality art program? Do you encourage student art exhibits, field trips and guest speakers as a part of your art program?

FINANCIAL SUPPORT: Does the school provide a separate budget for the art program other than student fees and donations from the PTA, PTO or some other source? Is there a budget for repair or replacement of materials, equipment and furniture for each classroom in which art is taught? Are there monies designated for professional development?

ART CURRICULUM: Do the written goals and objectives of your state, district and school include the study of art? Does the elementary art curriculum include the opportunity to produce creative artworks, to study art appreciation and history, art criticism and aesthetics? Is the curriculum sequential taking into account the developmental levels of children's art? Is the curriculum reviewed and revised every five years?

ART INSTRUCTION: Do teachers plan lessons and units in art which reflect the goals and objectives of the state and district curriculum? Are parents and students aware of the goals and objectives? Do teachers record pupil progress in art? Are teachers involved in the establishment of an appropriate evaluation of their teaching? Are students involved in the roles of artist, critic, historian and observer?

ART PERSONNEL: Is there one certified art teacher for every 350-450 children? If you do not have a certified art teacher, are the regular classroom teachers adequately trained to teach a variety of art activities and techniques, art appreciation and history, art criticism and aesthetics?

Leadership at the District Level

"Effective schools" leadership is also needed at the district level. An outstanding example of how this works is the Virginia Beach school district in Virginia, which maintains clearly defined district-wide policies, decision-making procedures, and expectations for each of its 62 schools. All instruction, including arts instruction, is based on curriculum guides prepared by district supervisors and teachers and backed by extensive resource materials.

Each major subject has a standing curriculum committee composed of teachers, supervisors, a school counselor, parents, and students. The committees meet for at least five days each year, during school time, to make recommendations on curriculum development and revision. Minutes from these committee meetings are circulated throughout the district and are available for public inspection.

PROFESSIONAL DEVELOPMENT: Is there an ongoing staff development program for your teachers? Are classroom teachers provided training in a variety of art activities and techniques, art appreciation and history, art criticism and aesthetics? Are the teachers pursuing advanced course work/degrees? Are the art teachers active members of their local, state and national art education associations?

TIME AND SCHEDULING: Do students receive art instruction from a certified art teacher or regular classroom teacher at least 100 minutes per week per year? If you have a certified art teacher, do the classroom teachers provide supplementary art experiences? Are class sizes consistent with the staffing ratio of other teachers in the building?

CLASSROOM MATERIALS AND RESOURCES: Are resource textbooks provided for each teacher? Are art textbooks provided for the students? Is there evidence that the teacher resource textbooks and student textbooks are being used? Are art films, filmstrips, slides, prints, posters, and original artwork available for teacher use? Does the library have a collection of resources for students on art activities and techniques, art appreciation, history and artists, careers in art, etc.? Are art magazines and journals available?

SUPPLIES AND EQUIPMENT: Are there consumable supplies for drawing, painting, sculpture, printmaking, ceramics, fibers, etc. readily available for teacher use? Do the students supply some of the art materials which can be brought from home at little or no expense to the students? Is your school equipped with specialized art equipment such as art furniture, sinks, kiln, paper cutter, tables, hand tools, etc.?

Source: National Art Education Association, *Quality Art Education: A Checklist Developed for Elementary Principals,* National Art Education Association, Reston, VA, undated.

The new Virginia Beach visual arts curriculum guide, which added art history and appreciation to art creation, was resisted by some of the visual arts teachers who had previously taught only craft skills. A few of these teachers were even placed on probation because their teaching did not reflect the district curriculum, but they were also given in-service training to help them develop teaching that would. A recent survey reveals that over 90 percent of the district's art teachers are now in favor of the district requirements. Most important, the survey also shows that district-wide adherence to a broad curriculum has resulted in higher student achievement, as most of a sample of the district's students scored several times higher than the national average on test questions taken from the National Assessment of Educational Progress visual art exam.

Beyond Creating: The Place for Art in America's Schools, a study released by the Getty Center for Education in the Arts in 1985, affirms that written, sequential curricula are crucial to effective teaching and learning in the visual arts. This finding contradicts the longstanding belief that visual arts teachers should seek to stimulate creativity without being bound by curricular constraints. The Virginia Beach teachers have reported on questionnaires, and demonstrated in their teaching, that the new curriculum allows ample room for instructional innovation.

The commitment and initiative of the district superintendent and his staff were key to implementing the Virginia Beach program. The superintendent made sure that everyone understood that the arts were to have the same status as any other school subject, and central office administrative and supervisory staff and school principals were given the challenge and the responsibility to make this happen, thereby creating an inspiring model. In *Art History, Art Criticism, and Art Production* (vol. 2), the investigator attributed the success of the Virginia Beach district to the superintendent's leadership:

> If all school districts were so well organized, so efficiently and effectively administered, and so enlightened concerning both their general educational program and the value they place on the role of art in that program, then art education in this country would rest on solid footing. As it now stands, basic changes in American art education would probably have to be preceded by changes in both the values and the administrative practices of school superintendents, their staffs, and school principals (p. 7-42).

Leadership at the State Level

State leadership in arts education manifests itself in many ways: in setting standards for the accreditation of college and university teacher training programs, standards for teacher certification, requirements for high school graduation and for subjects which must be taught in each grade, and requirements for entrance to state-administered colleges and universities. State leadership is also involved in adopting courses of study, curriculum frameworks and guides, and textbooks. State building-code requirements, health and safety requirements, and limitations on class size for educational as well as safety reasons also affect the classroom, as does legislation governing the negotiations between boards of education and unions. Finally, state legislation affects the budgets available to schools while state referenda can limit the authority of local taxing bodies to provide funding.

In a 1985 survey of state education policies and practices that support the arts, the Council of Chief State School Officers (CCSSO) found that:

- Forty-two states mandate arts instruction in elementary, middle or secondary schools.

- Thirty-six state education agencies had a state-level organizational unit for one or more of the arts, with music or visual arts included in every case.

- Nearly all of the states and special jurisdictions (50) employed arts specialists.

- There appeared to be more support for arts education from a functional than from a policy perspective in that only 13 states reported that their boards of education specified the arts within formal statements of educational goals, although 44 indicated they were in the process of revising policies in ways that would affect arts education positively.

- Forty-three states distribute guidelines for arts instruction to local districts, although these suggestions are usually general rather than specific.

- A majority of states (36) publish guidelines for visual arts and music; 20 states have guidelines in dance, drama, and creative writing, but only 12 states require that dance and/or drama be offered at the secondary level.

While states have increased their high school graduation requirements in the arts, most do not collect data on how effective their arts programs are or on how they are supported financially, whether from federal block grants, state categorical funds or discretionary income. Apparently, the trend is toward increased state support for arts education, although actual amounts vary considerably. State guides for curriculum adoption and state provision for textbook adoption can be a prescription for failure unless they are accompanied by corresponding technical support and adequate funding.

Nonetheless, the CCSSO report emphasizes the importance of state leadership in improving arts education, particularly when it is supported by state and local commitment:

> The majority of the SEA [state education agency] respondents believed that the formulation of new policies at the state level will lead to improved arts instruction in the state. They emphasized that legislative funding was a critical factor to the effective implementation of policies, and that such policies should define the arts as basic to the K-12 curriculum. They also recommended a commitment, both at the state and local level, to fund and otherwise enable schools to provide qualified instructors to teach the arts (in all subject areas), to offer sufficient numbers of courses to reach all students, and to ensure that the arts are included as part of solid academic preparation for a well-rounded, pre-collegiate education. In summary, respondents believed that if state and local administrators, teachers, and parents generally came to believe that the arts were basic, many of the problems encountered in providing quality comprehensive arts education for all students would in fact be resolved (pp. 6-7).

Although the states are generally responsible for all education, they exercise this function very differently. In the case of arts education, some legistate mandatory minimum requirements while others pass the responsibility to local school districts.

North Carolina is a good example of centralized state control. In 1984, North Carolina audited its entire educational curriculum under its Elementary and Secondary School Reform Act of 1984, and then in 1985 promulgated a 526-page *North Carolina Standard Course of Study*, a North Carolina *Competency-Based Curriculum*, and an 870-page teacher handbook on arts education. These reforms are to be implemented by the 1992-93 school year, with school accreditation eventually depending on compliance with them. There are also plans for a statewide program of testing to determine the success of the reform effort.

Colorado represents a good decentralized example. Colorado has no statewide curriculum requirements, no statewide curriculum guides or course of study, no state-adopted or mandated textbooks, no statewide standards for testing, no statewide test, and no statewide requirements for high school graduation (*Arts in the Schools: State by State,* 1985, p. 18).

Most states fall somewhere in between and responsibility for determining the character of arts programs may legitimately reside at any level. In some, the local school districts must either develop their own curriculum, or, as frequently happens, pass the responsibility on to the local school administrator who may in turn delegate it to individual arts teachers.

In other states, regional, county or intermediate educational agencies assist local school districts by providing programs and services which small districts would be unable to provide alone. In addition to coordinated purchasing and other administrative tasks, these agencies often provide leadership in curriculum development, staff development, and assistance with special populations.

State Leadership by Higher Education

Colleges and universities help arts education at the state level in many ways. Best known is their role in educating teachers. But they also encourage arts education research, and provide residencies for visiting artists and scholars. In addition, university museums exhibit works of art from their own collections and from touring exhibitions and sometimes prepare exhibits for use in schools. Campus performing arts facilities produce or present both home-grown and touring performances. Campus radio and television stations provide a variety of artistic fare to the community and state as well as hands-on instruction to students. Higher education staff often serve as consultants to state departments of education, local school districts, and the business-producer sector which provides materials for use in classrooms.

Finally, colleges and universities have direct impact on high schools through their entrance requirements and the courses for which they give credit. In too many cases, colleges and universities do not give credit for high school arts courses, concluding that the content of these courses does not meet their standards. An exception is the California State University system which, beginning in the fall of 1988, will require all incoming high school graduates to have successfully completed one year of visual or performing arts.

State Certification of Arts Teachers and Accreditation of School Programs

States are also responsible for setting standards for teacher training programs, the certification of teachers, and the effectiveness of certain categorical programs and services.

Teacher training institutions — public, private, and parochial — must meet state criteria if they offer students course work which leads to teacher certification. A recent trend shows a growing number of states requiring teacher candidates to pass qualifying examinations as well as successfully complete required course work. While standards vary from state to state, most states have certification standards for secondary art and music teachers. On the other hand, only 24 states have certification programs for theater and only 15 for dance teachers. And only 19 states require prospective arts teachers to pass qualifying examinations before receiving a certificate.

Standards for the preparation of arts teachers are also affected when colleges and universities voluntarily agree to have these programs reviewed and accredited by one of the four national accrediting associations — the National Association of Schools of Art and Design, the National Association of Schools of Dance, the National Association of Schools of Music, and the National Association of Schools of Theatre.

Thomas Jefferson, *Monticello*, the West Front and Gardens, Thomas Jefferson Memorial Foundation, Inc., James Tkatch

Many state departments of education also review K-12 school programs and accredit or approve them when they meet specified standards and comply with state regulations. In addition, schools can voluntarily agree to have their programs accredited by one of six regional accrediting associations which cover school programs in all subjects including the arts. Most regional associations develop standards to be used during a self-study process; this is followed by a site visit from an evaluation team. Unfortunately, regional association standards in the arts are usually too general to be very effective.

Leadership at the National Level

Leadership at the national level affects the climate for arts education. The U.S. Department of Education, the national professional associations of educators and education administrators, and several prominent not-for-profit entities are all key players.

U.S. DEPARTMENT OF EDUCATION

Although the federal government has no specific constitutional responsibility for education and provides only 9 percent of the money spent on education, the U.S. Department of Education can exert substantial influence through its support of state departments of education and of research. Unfortunately, the Department has not consistently provided broadly based support for research and curriculum development in arts education, and since 1979 art and music have not been part of the National Assessment of Educational Progress which it sponsors, although assessments of both had been planned at six-year intervals. Because other school subjects have been placed in the national spotlight and the arts have not, federal funding policies may have contributed to the perception that the arts are not as important as other school subjects.

Several recent developments are, however, encouraging. The 1983 report to the U.S. Department of Education by the Commission on Excellence in Education, *A Nation at Risk*, included the arts as one of the key components of the curriculum of the eight years leading to high school, and contended that the high school curriculum "should also provide students with programs requiring rigorous effort in subjects that advance students' personal, educational, and occupational goals, such as the fine and performing arts."

U.S. Secretary of Education William J. Bennett has been a strong voice in strengthening both arts and humanities education. In his 1986 report on elementary education, *First Lessons*, he declared that the "arts are an essential element of education, just like reading, writing, and arithmetic." This was helpful, as was his address to the annual meeting of the National Association of Schools of Music that same year when he said: "Not only do the arts contain an important part of what it means to be human, the arts also give coherence, depth, and resonance to other academic subjects. One of the primary tasks of our schools should be to train our young people to know, love, and respond to the products of the human spirit in music, dance, drama, and the visual arts. Surely it should be possible for them to emerge from their years of schooling with their eyes, ears, heads, and hearts attuned to what is lastingly beautiful in their cultural heritage."

In December 1987, Secretary Bennett issued a booklet presenting his idea of a core curriculum for American high school students. He described that report, *James Madison High School: A Curriculum for American Students,* as "an effort to spell out the essential elements of what all students should learn. It gives flesh to the minimum graduation requirements called for by *A Nation at Risk*." Most significant, Secretary Bennett's recommended high school curriculum requires one year in the fine arts — one semester in art history and one semester in music history. In addition, the report affirms that: "Studio arts, drama, and vocal and instrumental music are valuable and appropriate student pursuits; many secondary schools will want to offer them for credit as elective classes."

This recommendation, while not as broad as our recommendation for two years of study in the arts, would be an advance for the many states which have yet to generate arts requirements, per se. Consistent with these statements, the U.S. Department of Education has joined with the National Endowment for the Arts in funding research in arts education. On October 14, 1987, the Department and the Endowment jointly announced the establishment of research centers in arts education and in literature education.

This project, which is part of an overall U.S. Department of Education effort involving the content of the basic subjects in the K-12 curriculum, is particularly important in the arts, both symbolically and substantively. It is important symbolically because it represents an ongoing national collaboration between the Department of Education and the Arts Endowment; it also highlights the Department of Education's recognition that the arts should be as basic a part of education as English, math, and science. It is important substantively because there is perhaps less consensus on the nature of the arts curriculum than on that for other subjects.

In another collaborative effort with both the Arts Endowment and the Humanities Endowment, the U.S. Department of Education funded and fielded in 1987 a survey of a sample of school districts about their policies and programs concerning arts and humanities education. This survey was initiated as part of the "cooperation" Congress requested from the Department in developing the present report, which includes a substantial amount of that information.

The Education Department also continues to fund the education programs of the Kennedy Center for the Performing Arts ($3.3 million in Fiscal Year 1987), as well as Very Special Arts (a program affiliated with the Kennedy Center), which develops programs to integrate the arts into the general education of disabled children and the lives of disabled adults.

PROFESSIONAL ASSOCIATIONS AND MEMBERSHIP ORGANIZATIONS

In a country where formal responsibility for education rests at state and local levels, the national perspectives of the professional education associations are important to improving arts education. Four major groups of professional organizations influence arts education — associations of arts teachers in schools, associations of arts educators in higher education, associations of education administrators, and general associations of educators.

The objectives of the professional associations of arts teachers are to promote and improve arts education and provide a means for communication of ideas in the field. The most significant of these are the Music Educators National Conference, the National Art Education Association, the National Dance Association, the Music Teachers National Association, the American Association of Theatre for Youth, and the National Council of Teachers of English.

These associations work with public and private school teachers of the arts, arts supervisors and administrators, museum and arts institution educators, college professors of the arts, researchers and evaluators, arts advocacy organizations, and representatives of the private sector. They pursue their objectives through research, conferences, and publications.

Associations representing professional educators in higher education are also important. These include the National Association of Schools of Music, the National Association of Schools of Theatre, the National Association of Schools of Dance, the National Association of Schools of Art and Design, and the International Council of Fine Arts Deans.

These associations help develop a sense of common endeavor among their members, provide for accreditation, and set standards for granting academic credit, degrees, and other professional credentials. In January 1986, a consortium of arts educators (arts teachers and educators in higher education) concluded in a briefing paper for the arts education community, entitled *K-12 Arts Education in the United States: Present Context, Future Needs,* that arts educators needed "an action agenda" to develop "individual knowledge and skills in the arts in an increasing number of students" as well as "public understanding that art has important intellectual content as well as emotional appeal" (p. 32). In November 1986, in response to the revision of the Arts in Education guidelines of the National Endowment for the Arts, the same consortium published another briefing paper to encourage arts educators to work in partnership with state arts agencies to advance serious study of the arts in schools.

The Council of Chief State School Officers (CCSSO) has been particularly active in its support for arts education. Representing the commissioners and superintendents of education of the 50 states and seven special jurisdictions, the CCSSO's survey of state arts education policies was published in 1985 as *Arts, Education, and the States.* That same year the CCSSO convened a meeting on arts education attended by 27 commissioners and superintendents which reviewed the preliminary results of the survey and discussed the various issues in arts education. The survey and conference were sponsored by the U.S. Department of Education, the National Endowment for the Arts, and the Rockefeller Foundation.

In August 1985, the CCSSO published a catalogue of relevant state projects, *Options and Opportunities in Arts Education,* and expressed the hope that the catalogue would serve as a "catalyst for the development, expansion, or refinement of state initiatives in arts education across the country." In addition, the CCSSO Instruction Committee adopted 10 recommendations on arts education in 1985. These included establishing the arts as "part of the core of learning" and setting formal state education goals to allocate adequate funds to support arts education, provide quality arts instruction through qualified teachers, and incorporate the arts into state assessment and evaluation programs.

The National School Boards Association (NSBA), representing state associations in 50 states and two special jurisdictions, also actively supports arts education. The NSBA's strong support for integrating the arts "into the curriculum as essential elements" has been reiterated as recently as September 1987 in its publication, *Updating School Board Policies.* The lead article by Robert R. Spillane, Superintendent of Fairfax County (Virginia) Public Schools, declared: "Arts Education is not a frill! The arts are basic and essential." The NSBA has launched a joint annual awards program to honor local school boards for outstanding support of the arts in education. The first presentation occurred in March 1988.

The Board of the Association for Supervision and Curriculum Development (ASCD) represents approximately 90,000 teachers, administrators and other officials at every level of education. It adopted the following resolution at its 1985 annual meeting: "As a result of mounting graduation requirements in such fields as mathematics, science, and English, the arts have been frequently excluded from the general requirements. The arts are essential to student cognitive and affective growth and, therefore, should be a vital part of the required curriculum." And, in 1987, ASCD dedicated an entire issue of its journal, *Educational Leadership,* to the topic of arts education.

Still another example of the help arts education receives from professional associations is the collaboration between the American Association of School Administrators and the Alliance for Arts Education at the Kennedy Center for the Performing Arts. In 1985, these organizations coproduced a "how-to pamphlet," *Performing Together: The Arts and Education,* which presented a rationale for the central place of the arts in the schools and offered guidance for improving arts education.

The American Federation of Teachers (AFT) and the National Education Association (NEA), and their affiliated state and local unions, have also been supportive of arts education. In 1987, the National Education Association resolved that "artistic expression is basic to an individual's intellectual, aesthetic and emotional development" and that "every elementary and secondary school curriculum must include a balanced, comprehensive and sequential program of fine arts instruction taught by teachers certified in those fields." It has also urged its state affiliates "to become involved in the promotion, expansion and implementation of a fine arts program in the curriculum."

In 1988, the Executive Council of the American Federation of Teachers passed a resolution stating that:

> . . . the basic school curriculum, K-12, as a part of a balanced course of study in the arts, sciences and humanities, should require all students to study the arts. Students should be required to study the literary arts; the visual arts including design and architecture; the performing arts including music, dance, opera and theater; and the media arts in order to ensure that all students will be able to develop their creative potential and graduate from high school with a basic understanding of their society and of civilization.

Another organization which supports the arts as part of basic education is the College Entrance Examination Board (College Board). In 1983, the College Board included the arts as one of the six "basic academic subjects" for college preparation as a part of its Educational Equality Project, *Academic Preparation for College: What Students Need to Know and Be Able to Do.* In 1985, it followed up with a series of booklets on each of the six basics, including *Academic Preparation in the Arts.* Over 400,000 copies of *Academic Preparation for College* were sold or distributed, and over 25,000 copies of *Academic Preparation in the Arts* were sold (chiefly to schools and teachers).

The College Board reports that 23 states have taken some form of action in response to the recommendations in the booklets and that the National Urban League is translating the recommendations into workshop programs for parents and community organizations. By late 1988, the College Board will publish the results of a national survey measuring the degree to which its recommendations have been adopted, at which point a third generation of booklets will be published. The College Board has also included the arts among the basic academic subjects in its workshops for teachers. During the 1986-87 school year, some 3,000 teachers participated in 50 arts education workshops across the country.

THE ARTS SECTOR

While the arts have a very insecure place in the curriculum of most school districts, no other school subject has elicited such a broad network of support and advocacy from its practitioners. The arts sector may have no authority over the schools, but its members work tirelessly to strengthen arts education in the schools and to press its importance. Support comes in the form of influence, people, programs, and finance.

Artists and Arts Professionals

Today, approximately 8,200 practicing artists work in over 10,000 schools in residencies lasting from one day to a full school year. Often they are advocates for arts education and help teachers with the development of arts classes, particularly where no specialist teachers are available. In addition to working with small groups of students in class settings, artists-in-residence may give concerts or help with the creation of a mural or the printing and binding of a collection of poems. They also help young people learn how to be members of an audience and to see how an artist practices his or her craft. They also reach out to the community and help make it realize the importance of both the arts and arts education.

Some of America's best and most successful artists strongly believe in arts education and have devoted considerable time and energy, not to mention money, to working with young people. Arthur Mitchell, the first Black to become a *premier danseur* with the New York City Ballet, resigned from the company after the assassination of Martin Luther King to found a dance school which would attract young Blacks to the dance profession. The resulting Dance Theater of Harlem and its school continue to draw many of their students from Harlem and other economically deprived neighborhoods.

While still a principal with the New York City Ballet, Jacques d'Amboise founded the National Dance Institute to bring dance to schoolchildren in the New York City area. Each year Mr. d'Amboise and his trained assistants teach elementary school children in four or five

Martha Graham, photograph by Barbara Morgan, courtesy of the Martha Graham Dance Company, New York

selected schools for an entire school year. Their aim is not to recruit future professionals but to convey the joy and discipline of dance to children who would not otherwise experience it. The project is being copied in Boston and San Francisco with Mr. d'Amboise, who attracts children like a latter-day Pied Piper, closely supervising both efforts.

Bruce Marks, a former principal dancer with the American Ballet Theatre and the Royal Danish Ballet, currently artistic director of the Boston Ballet, is committed to reaching out to the community and providing arts education to the young. Having noticed that few minority dancers were interested in training in dance, he began in 1984 to work with two neighborhood elementary schools on the fourth and fifth-grade level for the purpose of exposing them to all kinds of dance — ballet, jazz, Spanish dance, African Black dance, and Chinese dance. In the 1987-88 school year, his program will reach 235 students.

Among the many musicians who have been active in arts education, Leonard Bernstein is perhaps best known for the televised young people's concert series he produced while he was director of the New York Philharmonic in the 1950's and '60's. His explanations of the workings of a symphony orchestra and brilliant interpretations of important symphonic works attracted huge audiences of young people.

Folk artists, whose work is based on traditions that stretch far into the past, are understandably concerned with the importance of keeping these traditions alive for new generations. Theo Bikel and Pete Seeger, for instance, have both worked with young people. Until her recent death, the great Bessie Jones devoted most of her time to working in Georgia's public schools to teach children the Black work songs and spirituals which she had done so much to preserve.

Cultural Institutions, Organizations, and Associations

Many art museums, art centers, theaters, and other cultural institutions have arts education programs. Their number is growing, and their influence can be national, regional, or local in scope. The arts sector also has countless membership and advocacy organizations, such as the American Council on the Arts, that can and do play important parts in advancing arts education. Since film, television, radio, and recordings are the cultural forms which most affect our young people, the organizations which produce and distribute them must be taken into account in designing arts education programs. They have enormous potential to contribute much more than they now do.

ORCHESTRA HALL
Wednesday, April 8 at 7:30 pm
CHICAGO NEW MUSIC ENSEMBLE
90th

Visual Arts and Design

Most art museums, whether large or small, sell or rent reproductions of works of art, films, books, and catalogues. Most provide education programs used by schools, including docent services for visiting school classes and assistance to classroom teachers in tailoring these visits to the curriculum. Many museums also offer teacher training, sometimes with local college or university credit.

Museums with national constituencies, like the National Gallery of Art in Washington and the Metropolitan Museum of Art in New York, have low-cost arts education programs with national constituencies. They distribute kits containing slides, workbooks, teaching guides, and other materials about individual artists, artistic periods or movements, or about more general historical subjects, such as "China: 1000 Years of Art and Culture" or "Arms and Armor." The Secondary Education Department of the Smithsonian Institution also distributes teaching kits about science, history, and the visual arts to thousands of schools across the country.

The J. Paul Getty Trust's Center for Education in the Arts began in 1981 a major effort to study and improve education in the visual arts. It has initiated several research efforts and a variety of pilot and demonstration projects in Discipline Based Art Education (production, history, criticism, aesthetics). Its Institute for Educators in the Visual Arts, a five-year pilot program involving 21 school districts, is designed to help elementary school classroom teachers teach the visual arts. The Getty Center has also provided $20,000 planning grants to eight regional institutes involving consortia of universities, school districts, and art museums in Florida, Minnesota, Nebraska, Ohio, Pennsylvania, Rhode Island, Tennessee, and Texas. It has funded school district planning grants in Provo, Utah; Robinsdale, Minnesota; and Portland, Oregon and is assisting three curriculum development institutes to provide model lesson plans in the hope of stimulating the interest of commercial publishers in creating materials for discipline-based arts education.

The architecture and design communities have undertaken a number of projects to provide students in elementary, middle, and secondary schools with a better sense of these disciplines. The American Institute of Architects Foundation has sponsored a "Sixth Grade Student Design Program" to introduce students to the design process. In a particularly interesting program in Broward County, Florida, the local AIA chapter has since 1983 sponsored K-12 student design competitions.

The Performing Arts

Performing arts institutions — symphony orchestras, choruses, theaters and dance companies — also have educational programs. Many give special performances and workshops in schools. In rural areas, these may offer schoolchildren their first chance to attend a live performance.

Young Audiences, with 37 chapters across the country, trains and sends professional artists into schools, and currently reaches almost five million children, or one of every eight. The Alliance for Arts Education of the John F. Kennedy Center for the Performing Arts promotes arts education through a network of committees now active in 41 states. The Lincoln Center Institute holds training workshops for teachers whose classes are invited to dress rehearsals or performances at Lincoln Center, a program that has been replicated in a number of cities outside New York. The Los Angeles Performing Arts Center trains teachers in summer institutes, offers quality arts residency programs, and provides performances in schools through its "Music Center on Tour" program.

Performing arts membership organizations like the American Symphony Orchestra League, OPERA America (an association of opera companies), Chamber Music America, Dance/USA, and the American Association of Theatre for Youth all have programs to introduce children to the art form with which they are concerned.

Creative Writing

The Teachers & Writers Collaborative sends professional writers into schools to work with teachers and students, and publishes materials relating to the teaching of writing. A number of school systems have organized "poets-in-the-schools" residencies with the Collaborative.

The Media

The most pervasive influence of the arts sector on young people's perception of art and culture comes through the communication media — television, publishing, recording, radio, and film. The most potent of these is television. Young people spend more time in front of the television set than in class — over six hours a day.

The television and other entertainment industries provide young people with a substantial portion of their regularly used vocabularies, including their vocabularies in the arts. Young people with only a vague idea of who Mozart was (unless they happened to see the movie version of *Amadeus*) will know all about Michael Jackson and Kenny Rogers. They will have a better sense of the language and rhythms of "Miami Vice" than those of Dickens, whose vocabulary is now often considered "too difficult" for average students.

These observations are not meant to imply that Michael Jackson is in the same league as Mozart or that Crockett and Tubbs are today's equivalent of Oliver Twist. It is to say that pop music and popular TV series (which often contain a great deal of music) cannot be ignored by those who would provide education in the arts. To do so would be to forfeit credibility among those young people whose confidence must be gained if they are to "get into" the wealth of art produced over time.

The wares of the popular media, however, are viewed by many educators (and artists and arts professionals) as of no educational account, and so no attempt is made to teach young people about the good and bad of popular culture. Yet, how can a young person understand what makes great art great without reference to the good and the bad of the popular arts that pervade the atmosphere?

Were young people better able to distinguish good from bad in popular culture, they might influence what the media give them, since the media respond to what audiences demand. But audience demand for a wider variety of fare depends on acquiring, through learning, a taste for different experiences, and that in turn depends upon acquiring the ability to understand the more complex vocabularies (even when extremely simple in exposition) of great art.

Those involved with the media are rarely viewed as leaders and educators, but they do in fact lead and educate outside the schools. Targeting audiences and developing products for them is a form of leadership, like it or not. Leadership may not be altruistic, and artists and educators may not like what it is selling, but young people and adults buy it and buy it freely. Hence, the offerings of television and the other media are major parts of actual education. The very fact that they are extracurricular and are consumed outside school adds to their attraction for many young people.

At the same time, the media have enormous power to improve education in the arts. Occasionally they do. The Leonard Bernstein young people's concerts on CBS begun in the '50's brought classical music to millions of young people. One reason Maestro Bernstein was so successful was that he made music from an earlier era relevant to young people, with periodic allusions to such popular music idols as the Beatles.

Given the influence of television, and its success via public television in teaching young people basic scientific principles in "3-2-1 Contact," the National Endowment for the Arts joined the John Paul Getty Trust in funding the development of a television series aimed at encouraging young people (ages eight-10) at home to become interested in the arts and gain some basic understanding of their principles. The hope is to educate in the arts without losing the child's attention; at home, it is easy simply to switch channels. The results of three pilot programs (in visual art, music, and dance) are expected in mid-1988. Written materials, which can be used in schools, will be prepared for each program.

Public television has taken its mission to present the arts very seriously, and it remains the main vehicle through which the television audience, children and adults, are given access to the arts. This fills a large gap, especially for those who lack geographical or financial access to live performances.

In helping to provide this access, the Arts Endowment and its sister agency, the Humanities Endowment, have played significant roles. NEH has supported the "American Short Story," and both agencies have contributed to an unprecedented poetry series, "Visions and Voices," of particular interest to high school students. "Live From Lincoln Center," "American Playhouse," "Dance in America," and "America By Design," all supported by the Arts Endowment, have consistently drawn audiences around the three million mark — low by commercial standards, but a vast extension of the arts audience for a particular event.

The influence of television is such that a single program, commercial or noncommercial, such as *"The Nutcracker"* or *"Amahl and the Night Visitors,"* can help stimulate increased interest in live performances of dance or opera. The challenge is to sustain this interest. The relatively new cassette technologies have opened major possibilities, including distributing cassettes about the arts to schools and libraries, though legal rights and distribution issues in this field must still be resolved.

The Role of Government in the Arts Sector

Another important segment of the arts sector is the federal, state, and local government agencies which subsidize the arts.

THE NATIONAL ENDOWMENT FOR THE ARTS

The National Endowment is the federal agency providing grants to artists and arts organizations across a diverse range of arts disciplines. The Endowment's Arts in Education Program is a $5 million program of grants to state arts agencies and other not-for-profit organizations specifically designed to help advance arts education in the schools. Further, grants to museums, orchestras, dance companies, theaters, and many other arts organizations help support artistic programs including those that reach young people. The next chapter, "The Role of the National Endowment for the Arts," discusses in detail Endowment policies, as well as its potential for helping to make comprehensive education in the arts available to all students.

STATE ARTS AGENCIES

All 50 states and the six special jurisdictions have arts agencies. Up to now their major education activity has been to administer artist residency programs for which the Endowment has provided financial support.

In Fiscal Year 1987, state and special-jurisdiction arts agencies spent an average of 9 percent of their state legislative appropriations on artists-in-residence programs. Individual state appropriations, however, ranged from as little as .85 percent to 35.3 percent. Twenty-two states spent 5 percent or less of their state legislative appropriations on artists-in-residence activities while 19 spent more than 10 percent, with four of the latter group spending 20 percent.

While residency programs remain the core of state arts agency arts education programs, over half the agencies are now engaged in planning activities, which include collaboration with state and local education agencies, to make the arts a more basic and sequential part of K-12 education. New initiatives in curriculum development, teacher and artist in-service training, evaluation procedures, and advocacy hold promise for the future. The National Assembly of State Arts Agencies (NASAA) published in 1988 an *Arts and Education Handbook: A Guide to Productive Collaborations*, which argues for an inclusive effort on the part of all elements in the arts and education sectors.

BUILDING STRONG COALITIONS: Minnesota State Arts Board

The Minnesota Comprehensive Arts Planning Program (CAPP) is an excellent example of the leadership coalition that exists between the Minnesota State Arts Board (MSAB), the Minnesota State Department of Education (MDE), and the Minnesota Alliance for Arts in Education (MAAE). CAPP was originally established in 1983 with $125,000 from state and private sources.

CAPP, in its third Biennium, aims to assist the development of a strong network of programming, planning, advocacy, and leadership in arts education throughout the state. In 1983, CAPP I, as it was then known, provided $125,000 to train local school arts leaders in 30 districts in the state and furnished the impetus for those educators to begin developing and implementing a well planned discipline-based arts curriculum for their students.

CAPP II began in 1985 with public/private partnership funding of $200,000 and was packaged together with a $4.9 million arts appropriation bill which included support for a Minnesota High School and Resource Center for the Arts and K-6 categorical arts education aid. The CAPP II program served 29 school districts throughout the state.

CAPP III is currently underway with a legislative appropriation of $150,000 and is serving 23 sites. Although the current biennial resources are less than in previous years, CAPP continues to exert a major influence in the development of arts education in Minnesota.

LOCAL ARTS AGENCIES

The first local arts agency was organized in 1949. By 1956, 55 were in existence, and by 1985 there were over 3,000. Nearly 750 of these agencies have professional staffs, and one-third receive some government funding, while the rest are private nonprofit organizations. Local arts agency budgets range from zero to $125 million (New York City). These community-based organizations serve as catalysts and planning entities to assist the community, arts institutions, artists, and schools in planning for and supporting the arts.

While much of this effort is focused on the adult population, there is a growing awareness that school-based arts education programs should be an important dimension of their efforts. For example, the 600-plus member National Assembly of Local Arts Agencies (NALAA) is developing a policy paper on arts education, and its 1987 survey of 305 NALAA members indicated that while the bulk of activity is in support of artist residencies and art classes or workshops outside of schools, a fifth to a quarter of the respondents are now engaged in advocacy and development of mandatory arts curricula in schools.

Advocates for Arts Education

The potential of the arts sector to advance arts education in schools is not yet being realized. Accustomed as the arts sector is to raising money, encouraging government support for the arts, and generally making the arts a part of community life, it has yet to rally behind the campaign to make the arts a basic and sequential part of the K-12 curriculum.

The National Endowment for the Arts, for example, has always expressed concern for arts education and funded state arts agencies to support artist residencies, but until the 1980's it did not try to encourage schools to make arts education a higher *educational* priority. The same is true of state art agencies which until recently did not venture beyond residency programs. By the same token, many artists and arts organizations have evolved their own arts education methods and even developed specific school programs, but generally they have not tried to change the way the education sector thinks about arts education.

In short, the arts sector has tended to let the education sector off the hook, thus contributing to the view that arts education can remain an extracurricular effort.

If the arts are to become a basic part of education, the education sector must become convinced of their educational, as well as their artistic worth. The arts sector can help with arts education, but it must first convince the education sector that not only is arts education in the education sector's interest, it is as essential to a satisfactory American education as English, math, and science. To do this, the arts sector will need to join forces with arts teachers to convince the rest of the

Excerpts from Brochure for Ad Hoc National Arts Education Working Group in 1987

AD HOC NATIONAL ARTS EDUCATION WORKING GROUP

On March 24, 1986 at the offices of the Pew Memorial Trust, the American Council for the Arts (ACA) and Music Educators National Conference (MENC) brought together leaders from twenty-five national organizations involved with arts education to discuss their common areas of interest. These leaders represented arts service organizations, arts advocacy groups and arts education associations. During the course of the day-long meeting the group drafted the "Philadelphia Resolution" reprinted here.

At subsequent meetings the resolution was refined and taken to the boards of each of the organizations for their approval. This group, the Ad Hoc National Arts Education Working Group, . . . continues to meet . . . to discuss major policy issues of the arts education field.

In the course of the meetings the group drafted and revised a second document, "Concepts for Strengthening Arts Education in School." The boards of directors of the groups have at this point adopted this second document.

The Ad Hoc Arts National Arts Education Working Group will continue to meet to further define the policy needs of the arts education field and to examine ways that this policy work can affect the improvement of arts education in local communities and the development of state arts education plans.

The group has been chaired by Fred Lazarus IV, President of the Maryland Institute College of Fine Arts, and co-convened by Milton Rhodes, President of ACA, and John Mahlmann, Executive Director of MENC.

PHILADELPHIA RESOLUTION, *March 24, 1986*

WHEREAS, American Society is deeply concerned with the condition of elementary and secondary education; and

WHEREAS, the arts are basic to education and have great value in and of themselves and for the knowledge, skills and values they impart; and

WHEREAS, the arts are a widely neglected curriculum and educational resource in American schools; and

WHEREAS, numerous national reports have cited the arts as one of the most basic disciplines of the curriculum; and

WHEREAS, every American child should have equal educational opportunity to study the arts as representations of the highest intellectual achievements of humankind;

THEREFORE, the undersigned individuals, representing a broad cross-section of national arts organizations, agree:

THAT EVERY elementary and secondary school should offer a balanced, sequential, and high quality program of instruction in arts disciplines taught by qualified teachers and strengthened by artists and arts organizations as an essential component of the curriculum;

THAT WE PROMOTE public understanding of the connections between the study of the arts disciplines, the creation of art, and development of a vibrant, productive American civilization;

THAT WE URGE inclusion of support for rigorous, comprehensive arts education in the arts development efforts of each community;

THAT WE PURSUE development of local, state and national policies that result in more effective support for arts education and the professional teachers and artists who provide it.

education sector that arts education, like other education, must include specific learning outcomes, be taught sequentially, and use testing to see if the teaching results in the stipulated outcomes.

To a degree, this is happening. For example, the American Council for the Arts has joined the Music Educators National Conference in building alliances among arts educators and the arts sector. The education sector must be convinced that arts education does not just consist in performances and exhibitions applauded by parents, but is valuable in and of itself.

The arts sector can do this. The trustees of orchestras, museums, and other arts organizations, and the many volunteers who help them, are usually civic leaders in their communities. They wield influence with their school boards, school superintendents, and members of state legislatures. They have already made substantial commitments to the cultural life of their cities and towns. If they were to devote a small portion of this energy to convincing the schools that education in the arts should be basic and sequential and that school time and money should be allocated to this end, school boards and schools would follow.

Advocacy by the arts sector for arts education is also in its own best interest. Future audiences for the arts outside the popular culture depend on their appreciation and understanding of those arts. So does future patronage of those arts. The Arts Endowment and state and local arts agencies can assist with these efforts, and they will, but ultimately the curriculum, and the resources and time allocated to it, will be determined by citizens in school districts. Those who know and love the arts and what they mean to the community must now take their case to the schools and to those who determine school policy, so that *all* Americans, not just the better educated or those going on to college, can have a sense of their civilization as represented in the best of art.

THE BUSINESS-PRODUCER SECTOR

The business-producer sector which affects arts education includes publishers of elementary and secondary school textbooks on the arts (both teacher and student editions); the writers, developers, and publishers of tests for students and teachers; and the suppliers of recorded music, reproductions of works of art, musical instruments, and band uniforms.

This sector helps to determine the arts curriculum in subtle ways that are sometimes not even recognized by arts educators. For example, if inexpensive high-quality reproductions of works of art from major periods and styles of art are unavailable, they are less likely to be studied.

Private-sector manufacturers of instructional materials are guided by the marketplace. But state departments of education can affect the marketplace by providing powerful incentives, particularly for textbook publishers. In a few key states, state boards of education approve lists of textbooks and materials from which school districts may select what they use. This procedure gives these states greater assurance that their curriculum guidelines will be supported by the instructional materials actually bought and used by local districts. The state lists are based on the recommendations of review committees in accordance with published criteria. In some cases, publishers are actually asked to review their materials so they will conform to the specific conditions of the state curriculum commissions.

Since textbooks are second only to teachers in determining the content of courses, editors of classroom texts, who successfully deal with state textbook adoption policies, have a powerful influence over what children learn. This is magnified by the current trend among educational publishers to develop not simply single texts on a particular subject area but complete "systems" of texts that stretch over several grade levels.

The power of the editors is further magnified when we consider that the largest states, where the biggest markets are located, may in effect set policies for smaller states since publishers tend to publish only those textbooks whose wide circulation is assured. A state which finds such a textbook unsatisfactory, for whatever reason, may be forced to order it because nothing better is available.

While central ordering of materials is characteristic of textbook sales, the converse is true of audio-visual resources, supplies, and computer software. These are usually purchased directly by the school from commercial producers. And, equipment and art supplies are bought in quantity to assure cost savings whenever possible. State policies are less specific with respect to these materials, and the schools have more control, primarily because of limited budgets for these kinds of resources.

It is ironic that in an age of television, control, funding, and attention are still overwhelmingly focused on the printed word. Audio-visual materials, which may have equal or stronger influence on students, are not made to conform to state and local education policies and objectives.

RECOMMENDATIONS

The governance, education, arts and business-producer sectors should work together to convince parents and political and education leaders at the state, district, and local levels that education is complete and acceptable only when the arts are included as essential components sequentially taught. Making the case for arts education to state and local leadership is a political job requiring greater effort than it does for school subjects that large segments of the public already perceive to be basic. To this end:

A. National, state, and local arts education advocates need (i) to develop greater consensus on the objectives of arts education—what students are expected to learn at what ages, (ii) to obtain official recognition of the importance of arts education from the highest levels of political leadership — and then (iii) to work cooperatively to plan for and implement effective programs in school districts and schools (as a part of general education reform).

B. The case for arts education should be made in the same way as for any other subject: i.e., for sequential and testable instruction by qualified teachers, with high school graduation requirements that specify the arts (not in the alternative with other subjects), and with adequate time, money, curricula, and materials.

C. State education and arts agencies should work cooperatively with regional and local education and arts agencies, professional organizations, artists and arts institutions to provide leadership and support for improving arts education.

D. At the local level, community leaders (in particular the trustees of arts organizations) should work with local school boards, parent-teacher associations and schools to ensure that the arts are in fact sequentially taught in schools by qualified teachers for *all* students (not just the gifted and talented).

E. Programs should be instituted to help local school board members and education administrators understand why it is their responsibility, and thus in their interest, to make arts education a priority. These programs should help local school board members and education administrators to provide leadership for this part, as for other parts, of the curriculum.

Charlie Chaplin in *The Kid*, courtesy of The American Film Institute, Washington

The Role of the National Endowment for the Arts

The goal of the National Endowment for the Arts in the area of education is to advance comprehensive and sequential education in the arts as a part of basic education in the schools. The Endowment pursues this goal primarily through its Arts in Education Program. Many of its arts discipline programs also fund educational projects both in and outside the schools. The Endowment's current work is described and evaluated in this chapter.

We also consider the educational role of the National Endowment for the Humanities and the National Science Foundation, our federal equivalents for the other two branches of education, as well as the work of the U.S. Department of Education (see Appendices A, B, and C, respectively).

THE ARTS IN EDUCATION PROGRAM

The Endowment's arts education effort began in 1966 as The Arts and Education three-year Laboratory Theater Project. The project was established in cooperation with the United States Office of Education (USOE) and state and local school boards to "develop new audiences of all ages and to improve the quality of secondary school instruction in dramatic literature by making live professional theater productions an integral part of high school curricula."

The Endowment then funded an Academy of American Poets program in which established poets gave readings for teachers to stimulate their interest in poetry, and in which younger, lesser-known poets read and discussed their poetry in high school classrooms. By the 1967-68 school year, these programs had reached cities in Arizona, California, Illinois, Minnesota, and New Mexico.

The Artists-in-Schools Program (AIS) was established in 1969 through a transfer of $100,000 from USOE to the Arts Endowment. It placed visual artists in residence in six school districts throughout the country. The project was administered by the Central Midwestern Regional Educational Laboratories (CEMREL).

An additional $900,000 was later transferred by USOE to the Endowment to expand the program to other states and to include the disciplines of dance, music, and theater. In 1971, USOE funds were replaced by $750,000 in Endowment funding, and by 1979 this amount was increased to $4.86 million. By the 1973-74 school year, AIS programs had been initiated in all 50 states and two of the six special jurisdictions.

In 1980, the program, renamed the Artists in Education Program, was expanded to provide for artist residencies in educational settings beyond schools and school systems. A Special Projects category was established to support projects to "demonstrate and further the knowledge of the value of the arts and artists in the education process."

In 1986, after extensive field consultation, research, and consideration by the National Council on the Arts, and with the encouragement of Congress during the Endowment's 1985 reauthorization, the program was refocused to encourage states and localities to make the arts a basic and sequential component of the school curriculum, from kindergarten through high school, while continuing support for artist residencies. The program was renamed the Arts in Education Program (AIE).

The Fiscal Year 1988 AIE program budget is $5.5 million for three funding categories:

1. **State Arts in Education Grants (SAEG)** ($3.4 million) are awarded to state arts agencies to support the placement of practicing artists of professional excellence in a wide variety of educational settings. Funds may also be used to support projects which make the arts a more basic and sequential part of education, including teacher in-service workshops, advocacy efforts, institutional collaborations, and development of sequential arts curricula.

In the 1986-87 school year, the Arts in Education Program funded 7,851 artists in residence in 11,187 sites in all 50 states and five special jurisdictions, reaching 3.5 million students and more than 116,000 teachers. Despite these efforts, it is estimated that artist residencies reach only approximately 10 percent of schools and are not for the most part integrated with curriculum instruction. But they have given many young people a chance to meet "real live" professional artists who can convey to them a sense of the creative process and give them a rare contact with original art. As several state arts agency representatives have pointed out, residencies have been a "foot in the door" for development of school support for regular instruction in the arts.

An artist residency program can have multiple effects. For example, in Fiscal Year 1986, the Endowment provided $163,900 to the Ohio Arts Council to support its artist residency program for the 1986-87 school year; the state matched this sum with $850,900. The program involved 127 artists, 51,355 students and other participants, and 1,688 teachers and administrators at 107 sites. Residencies were both long-term (five to 12 months) and short-term (two to three weeks). These residencies involved teachers and school administrators in in-service workshops. The Ohio program also has a Special Projects component to assist collaborations among schools and universities, museums, and community arts organizations. It funds 12 fellowships for arts teachers to pursue summer projects that enhance their artistic development.

2. **Arts in Schools Basic Education Grants (AISBEG)** ($1 million) are awarded to state arts agencies on a competitive basis. These grants encourage their collaboration with state and local education agencies in planning and developing a practical commitment to make the arts a basic and sequential part of education K-12. The AISBEG grants include a first phase of planning grants (up to $20,000) and a second phase of implementation grants (up to $50,000 a year for two to three years) to assist in making the arts education planning (developed with the help of the planning grants) operational.

Sixteen of the 42 states which applied in Fiscal Year 1987 received planning grants, and eight more are being funded in Fiscal Year 1988. Many of the Fiscal Year 1987 applicants which did not receive Endowment grants nevertheless proceeded with statewide planning in arts education. We expect more states to participate in this category in coming years.

The Maine State Commission on the Arts used its Fiscal Year 1987 grant to assist planning for the development in Maine of high-quality, comprehensive, and sequential arts education programs using the state's arts resources. Working with the state education agency and the Maine Alliance for Arts Education, the Commission is identifying model arts education programs and disseminating information about them to school administrators and teachers. It is also seeking funding and other resources to help schools and cultural organizations meet recently enacted state curriculum requirements making the arts both a high school graduation requirement and part of the basic course of study at the elementary level.

The Endowment's AISBEG planning support of $20,000 was matched with $63,000 in cash. To put its long-range plan into practice, the Maine Arts Commission is eligible in Fiscal Year 1988 for an implementation grant of up to $150,000 for three years.

3. **Special Projects Grants** ($1.1 million) are available to a wide variety of not-for-profit organizations such as educational institutions, arts institutions, and local arts agencies. They support projects which advance arts teaching as a basic part of education, K-12, and provide for Endowment leadership initiatives. Twenty-eight Special Projects grants in Fiscal Year 1987 were awarded for activities such as curriculum and teaching guide development and for teacher education.

In Fiscal Year 1987, this category also funded a joint initiative with the U.S. Department of Education to establish an Arts Education Research Center and a Center for the Learning and Teaching of Literature. First-year funding in a three-year plan is $807,000 for the Arts Education Center, and $500,000 for the Literature Center. The centers will undertake research and disseminate information and analysis concerning specific elements which should be part of the learning, teaching, and assessment of arts and literature education. They will work closely with the newly established Elementary Subjects Center, also funded by the U.S. Department of Education. The information developed by the centers will be made available to school districts and schools, universities, arts organizations, and parent and professional organizations.

DISCIPLINE PROGRAMS

Although the Arts Endowment has funded arts education initiatives largely through the Arts in Education Program, the educational activities of arts organizations are also eligible for support from the Endowment's discipline programs. The extent of funding has been determined by individual program priorities and by the quality of applications received. The following examples represent the kind of work funded.

Through its Media Arts Program, the Endowment has entered into an agreement with the J. Paul Getty Trust's Center for Education in the Arts to produce a television series on the arts for young people aged eight to 10 for home viewing, with instructional materials for use in schools. Pilot programs are now being produced and tested. A decision is expected in 1988 about proceeding with a full series. The Endowment has invested approximately $1.9 million to date on this effort, with funding coming primarily from the Media Arts Program.

The Folk Arts Program has funded projects to educate students about America's multi-ethnic traditions. The Expansion Arts Program has funded organizations such as Urban Gateways, which trains professional artists in all disciplines to work in schools in the eight-county metropolitan area of Chicago, and Concerned Musicians of Houston, which sponsors a "Jazz and Poetry" series in the public schools.

The Museum Program, under the Utilization of Museum Resources category, has funded a variety of educational projects. Examples are the Fiscal Year 1986 grant, in cooperation with the J. Paul Getty Trust Grant Program, to the Denver Art Museum to develop new labels, printed material, and audiovisual instructions for students, and a Fiscal Year 1987 grant to the International Center for Photography to compile a primer on photography for students aged eight to 15. In addition, many visual artists' organizations supported by the Endowment have outreach programs in neighborhood schools.

The Design Arts Program has supported a number of arts education projects including a kit compiled by the Boston Children's Museum to teach graphic design to young people, a Pittsburgh Architects Workshop to produce a workbook on design for high school students, and a project in Oakland, California to teach elementary pupils about urban planning.

The Inter-Arts Program supports a number of presenting organizations involved in education such as the Los Angeles Music Center and the Clearwater, Florida, Performing Arts Center and Theater, as well as two festivals specifically aimed at children in Philadelphia and Pittsburgh. The Dance Program supports dance companies, many of which have outreach programs in schools or mount special children's performances.

The Opera-Musical Theater Program supports companies like Opera/Omaha and the Midwest Opera Theatre and School in St. Paul, Minnesota, which take touring productions to the schools. It also helps the Michigan Opera Theatre-in-Residence program, which offers communities a full week of in-school performances, lecture demonstrations, master classes, and workshops.

According to the American Symphony Orchestra League, 79 percent of America's orchestras, many of which are supported through the Music Program, spend an estimated 11 percent of their budgets for young people's concerts, reaching an estimated 10 million students annually. An unusual example is the work of Strings for Schools, an arts organization which reaches some 62,000 children in rural southeastern Pennsylvania with chamber music concerts accompanied by commentary and slides. Affiliate Artists, Inc., based in New York, also receives Endowment funding to support its artist-residency program. Affiliate Artists brings singers and instrumentalists who are in the early stages of their careers into schools.

Regional theaters supported by the Theater Program often stage special performances for school groups, and many also provide special instructional materials to enhance the experience. Perhaps the most acclaimed student performance series are the "Discovery" program of the Trinity Repertory Theater in Providence, Rhode Island, and the New York Shakespeare Festival's "Shakespeare on Broadway," which stages Shakespeare presentations for schools in a rented Broadway theater.

Media Art Centers supported by the Media Arts Program have also brought outreach programs to schools in their vicinities. Multimedia, Inc., brings Chicago schoolchildren to its center for film viewings and discussion, and Film in the Cities, which has a similar program in Minneapolis-St. Paul, is currently developing a K-12 media arts curriculum.

The Literature Program has made awards to such notable writers' organizations as the Teachers and Writers Collaborative, which sends poets to public school classrooms all over New York City. It has also helped fund the Collaborative's Whole World Catalogue, a handbook for teachers of creative writing, which has been used since 1977 as a major national resource for writing teachers.

Deborah Butterfield, *Horse,* 1985, Hirshhorn Museum and Sculpture Garden, Smithsonian Institution, Washington

THE CHALLENGE PROGRAM

Since 1977 the Arts Endowment's Challenge Program has awarded more than $193 million in three-to-one "matching" grants to outstanding American institutions. Some of these have an educational focus. For example, a 1987 award of $150,000 will be used to establish an endowment fund for New York's Studio in a School, a unique visual arts program which enlists students, parents, and teachers to work in public elementary schools that have no formal arts programs. Earlier grants have included $100,000 to Boston's Cultural Education Collaborative, $200,000 to Young Audiences, Inc., and a major award of $650,000 to the Exploratorium in San Francisco.

In 1987, the Endowment created a new Challenge Program, Challenge III. One of its four components is to foster arts appreciation. The first awards under the new guidelines will be announced in October 1988. The specific targeting of appreciation projects— those seeking to develop "deeper and broader education in and appreciation of the arts"— creates a significant new opportunity for Endowment support of arts education. The program is open to a wide range of educational institutions, systems, or consortia, as well as arts organizations. Grants will range from $50,000 to $1 million and must be matched three to one. To serve the needs of organizations which are not yet competitive at Challenge Program levels, the Endowment's Advancement Program will also be opened to arts education for the first time in Fiscal Year 1990.

EVALUATION OF ENDOWMENT EFFORTS

Concern for arts education has always existed at the Arts Endowment, and the Endowment's efforts have been helpful in placing artists in schools and stimulating outreach on the part of arts institutions. But Endowment-supported projects relating to arts education were primarily conceived as helping artists and arts institutions rather than educating K-12 students. Until recently, they had not addressed the central issues involved in making the arts a basic and sequential part of the K-12 curriculum.

In 1978, the National Council on the Arts published a report on Endowment efforts in arts education. The general conclusion was that outside of AIE-funded artist residencies, the Endowment's efforts in education should be confined to assisting professional training in those fields where this was considered a priority.

But the Endowment's 1982 survey of its public participation in the arts caused this conclusion to be reappraised. According to this study, 61 percent of American adults had not in the preceding 12 months attended a single live performance of jazz or classical music, opera or musical theater, or ballet, nor visited a museum or gallery. The inference from this 1982 study was that the artistic efforts supported by the Endowment were not benefiting the majority of Americans. This led the Endowment to reevaluate its position on arts education and begin to consider activities which could over time make the artistic activities which it supported more a part of the lives of all Americans.

The initial efforts in this direction included consultation with representatives of the arts and education sectors across the country. On the basis of that consultation, a new AIE program was developed. While many of the state arts agencies which had been beneficiaries of Endowment funding of artist residencies were initially skeptical, the new program quickly became popular with the vast majority of states. For the first time, the Arts Endowment was able to enlist support from many elements in the education sector, particularly the associations which represent arts teachers.

The thrust of the new program is, first, to encourage collaboration among state and local arts and education organizations and agencies in making arts education integral to the school curriculum, and, second, to make the case to the governance and education sectors that basic and sequential arts education K-12 is not only in their interest, but most important, in the interest of the students and the nation.

This evolution of Endowment thinking, which began in 1983, was joined in 1984-85 by congressional concern for arts education. A hearing on the subject was held by the full Committee on Education and Labor in February 1984, and arts education was an important part of the Endowment's reauthorization hearings in 1985. The result of this congressional concern was twofold: the inclusion by Congress in the Endowment's basic purpose of a special provision regarding arts education in schools, and the congressional request for this report.

Although arts education is now receiving increased attention from the Endowment, it remains true that the Arts Endowment spends less time and money, as a proportion of its overall activities, on arts education than do its counterpart agencies, the National Endowment for the Humanities and the National Science Foundation, on K-12 humanities and science education. Only 3.3 percent of Arts Endowment funding is currently budgeted for support of education programs, compared with 12.8 percent of Humanities Endowment funding for humanities education and just over 5 percent of National Science Foundation funding for science education.

These differences derive from the fact that the Arts Endowment has traditionally focused on professional arts creation, production, presentation, exhibition, and preservation, rather than education. The Humanities Endowment and the National Science Foundation have, on the other hand, from their beginnings considered education as one of their principal priorities. These differences may stem in part from the perception that education in the humanities and sciences is necessary to understand, appreciate, and use them, while the "serious" arts, like entertainment, can be experienced without knowing anything about them.

Similarly, in the schools themselves, arts education has been primarily production and performance oriented. The emphasis has been on providing it to talented students rather than all students, on the implicit assumption that the general student can appreciate the arts simply by experiencing them. Education in the humanities and sciences, on the other hand, has always been considered necessary.

The very limited U.S. Department of Education funds for assisting development of the content of arts education have been devoted primarily to performance and production through support of such activities as the Kennedy Center's education programs. It should be noted, however, that when William Bennett became Secretary of Education, the Department's focus on the arts as a part of education changed. The Department now considers the arts to be a basic part of education, and it has joined the Arts Endowment in funding through the Office of Educational Research and Improvement a variety of efforts to assist the process of making them so.

In sum, the Arts Endowment from its beginnings in the 1960's has through both its Arts in Education and discipline programs funded a number of projects to provide arts resources for schools. But not until very recently has it attempted to change the attitudes of the schools and the general public toward the arts as educational essentials.

The Endowment's new efforts build on its earlier programs, but now seek, first, to change basic attitudes about the arts in education and, second, to provide information and models for the schools to use in moving forward with arts education as a basic and sequential part of the K-12 curriculum. While the Arts Endowment's traditional efforts on behalf of arts education were useful, they were also limited and did not address the basic difficulties confronting arts education in schools. The new Endowment efforts do address these difficulties, but their potential for *effectively* addressing them remains to be seen.

It is the conclusion of this report that Endowment resources for arts education, both staff and money, need to be enhanced and continued over a period of at least 10 years in order to gain a true sense of the effectiveness of this basic endeavor. The results of the Arts in Education Program's encouragement of collaboration, planning, and implementation of model programs in schools can be assessed only after a generation of students have benefited from them. Even if a particular school district were to implement Endowment-funded state and local planning with a series of curricular programs in 1989, it would be 13 years before the first student passed through all the grades containing those programs.

It is therefore this report's general recommendation that the current direction of the Arts in Education Program be continued and strengthened over the next decade, and that in preparation for reauthorization in the mid-'90's a second arts education report to the Congress be prepared. On this basis, the President and the Congress could evaluate progress.

CONCLUSION

The National Endowment for the Arts has an important and timely opportunity to influence the course of arts education. While it is not an education agency, the Endowment should pursue current initiatives and, to some degree, operate in the arts education area as do the National Endowment for the Humanities and the National Science Foundation in humanities and science education. Such a role would not necessarily require substantial additional funds for the Arts in Education Program, but it would require changing the way in which the Endowment functions vis-à-vis the other sectors of arts education.

It should be remembered that the National Endowment for the Arts is not an education agency and that decisions on learning goals, curricula, resources, and testing and evaluation are, and should be, ultimately made at the state and school-district levels. Nonetheless, the Endowment believes that it can and should exercise a leadership role in encouraging, in collaboration with state and local arts agencies and state and local education authorities, a more basic and sequential approach to arts education.

It cannot be stressed too much that reform in arts education must be undertaken on a long-term basis and measured in decades, not years. We know at this stage of no school district in the country that has included the arts in the curriculum systematically, comprehensively, and sequentially from kindergarten through twelfth grade. The task of restructuring and reforming arts education is therefore more difficult than for subjects traditionally included in the core curriculum.

RECOMMENDATIONS

The National Endowment for the Arts, which is to arts education what the National Science Foundation is to science education, should (i) make the case for arts education, (ii) facilitate collaboration among the four sectors concerned with arts education (governance, education, arts, business-producer) to make it a basic and sequential part of school instruction, and (iii) assist development and distribution of curricular, instructional, and assessment models for the benefit of state and local education authorities. To this end:

A. The policies and resources (staff and money) of the Endowment for arts education should be continued and strengthened over a period of at least 10 years in order to allow implementation of present policies and of the recommendations in this report to bear fruit. The Fiscal Year 1989 budget request for the Endowment's Arts in Education Program provides for such strengthening in that year.

B. The Endowment should provide the President and the Congress a report on progress in arts education in preparation for the Endowment's reauthorization in the mid-'90's (the reauthorization which follows anticipated reauthorization in 1990).

C. The Endowment should advocate the development of higher standards for state and local arts curriculum guides, courses, and curriculum materials. It should provide limited funding to assist state/local curriculum development. It should, in cooperation with the U.S. Department of Education, convene a meeting of experts to review curricular materials (including the work on curricula of the new national research centers on the arts, literature, and elementary subjects) with a view to making recommendations on arts curricula and on school programs to implement them.

D. The Endowment should work with the U.S. Department of Education to develop a plan for the inclusion of each of the arts in the National Assessment of Educational Progress. The plan should include analysis of whether arts education might best be assessed by (i) separate assessments for each of the individual arts, (ii) a general arts assessment, (iii) integrating arts assessments with other subject area assessments, or (iv) a combination of these.

E. The Endowment should provide limited funding to assist state-level development of model assessment plans, programs and procedures, both with respect to programs and student testing.

F. The Endowment should encourage (i) state education agencies and arts education associations to recruit highly qualified arts teachers; (ii) state certifying agencies to raise standards for teacher certification and teacher preparation programs accreditation; and (iii) school boards to hire qualified arts teachers. The Endowment should encourage the arts sector to lend support to these efforts.

G. The Endowment should continue to identify areas in which there is a need for systematic and regular collection of baseline survey data on arts education, and it should disseminate the results of its studies and data to the arts education communities and the public. The Endowment should also provide limited funding to assist efforts to translate research into classroom practice.

H. The Endowment should appoint an ongoing Advisory Board (with representatives of the governance, education, arts, and business-producer sectors) whose purpose would be to institute a national dialogue on:

> (i) what students, at a minimum, should know of and about the arts when they graduate from high school, (ii) how required course units might be structured to include teaching of these minimum requirements, and (iii) what evaluation mechanisms might be appropriate and effective to assess whether students have actually mastered such materials and skills.

The Advisory Board should specifically advise the Endowment on:

> (i) activities and efforts which it could undertake to ensure that the recommendations in this report are addressed by the appropriate parties, (ii) development (with appropriate agencies and associations) of proposals for a master plan for arts assessment as part of the National Assessment of Educational Progress, (iii) development of a plan by which exemplary school and district arts programs might be identified, recognized, and rewarded (e.g., exemplary schools, programs and teachers); and (iv) the report to the President and Congress suggested for the Endowment's mid-'90's reauthorization.

I. The Endowment should provide a national model for the kind of collaboration necessary to make progress in arts education. The model should in particular include the U.S. Department of Education, the National Endowment for the Humanities, and the national associations that can influence arts education. The Endowment should assist states, localities, and the arts education community generally to develop a clearer vision of what arts education in the United States can and should be.

APPENDIX A

National Endowment for the Humanities

The National Endowment for the Humanities (NEH) spends a considerably larger portion of its budget on programs to improve elementary and secondary humanities education than the Arts Endowment does with respect to arts education. In Fiscal Year 1988 NEH expects to spend a total of about $17.9 million (or 12.8 percent of its total budget) in support of humanities education in the schools. This support comes from three of NEH's funding divisions: the Division of Education Programs, the Division of Fellowships and Seminars, and the Division of State Programs.

In Fiscal Year 1988, the Division of Education Programs estimates obligations of $8.5 million to elementary and secondary education — $8 million for grants to support summer institutes, academic-year masterworks study, conferences, workshops, and related activities, and an additional $500,000 for a national history center to conduct research on effective approaches to the teaching of history in the schools. In the Division of Fellowships and Seminars, a total of $3.9 million has been allocated — $3.7 million for summer seminars for school teachers, and approximately $200,000 in grant support for high school students to conduct research and writing projects in the humanities. In the Division of State Programs, which provides support to state humanities councils in the 50 states and Puerto Rico and the Virgin Islands, NEH estimates that about $5.1 million will be devoted to seminars and institutes for teachers and school administrators and to other educational programs at the elementary and secondary levels.

Many of NEH's other programs also have an impact on humanities education at the precollegiate level. The Division of Research Programs, for example, funds basic research in the humanities disciplines, much of which will ultimately benefit teachers and students in elementary and secondary schools. And, the Division of General Programs provides support to museums, libraries, and television and radio stations for interpretive humanities programming for audiences of all ages.

APPENDIX B

National Science Foundation

The National Science Foundation (NSF) also spends more of its budget on science education than the Arts Endowment does on arts education. This conforms with NSF's enabling legislation of 1950 which authorizes and directs the Foundation "to initiate and support . . . science education programs at all levels in the mathematical, physical, medical, biological, social, and other sciences . . . and engineering education programs at all levels in the various fields of engineering."

NSF began research and education programming in Fiscal Year 1952 with $1.54 million of a total budget of $3.47 million. None of these funds, however, were dedicated to elementary or high school education. In Fiscal Year 1957, nonetheless, the appropriation for pre-college education jumped to $10.2 million from $850,000, accounting for over a quarter of the agency's budget. NSF's Fiscal Year 1988 budget provides $89.6 million (or 5.2 percent) for pre-college science education, including $45.2 million for pre-college teacher preparation and enhancement; $37.5 million for material development, research, and informal science education; $3.7 million for the "young scholars" program; and $3.2 million for studies and program assessment.

The Foundation's programs cover every educational level from kindergarten through postdoctoral studies. NSF's support of programs for students is usually indirect. Fellowship and research grants, however, go directly to graduate students. Programs for teachers and faculty members are both direct and indirect. The Foundation has not supported education facilities, but has supported and does support research facilities.

Direct teacher programs supported by NSF include summer or academic year institutes (designed to upgrade disciplinary knowledge and improve instructional effectiveness); fellowships or scholarships to support individual advanced study; projects to create new curricula for the preparation of school science and mathematics teachers; and support for the establishment and initial operation of teacher networks.

Indirect support to improve science and math instruction has included: projects to improve elementary school, middle school, high school, and college science and mathematics curricula; projects to create new high school and college science and mathematics courses; programs to develop new instructional methods, materials, and apparatus; support of science museums, radio and television programming, and other methods for accomplishing informal science and mathematics education; support for research on the processes of teaching and learning; and projects to gather longitudinal information on a variety of education-related topics including demographics and student achievement.

NSF targets specific student populations in undertaking these programs: those who are likely to enter one of the fields of mathematics, engineering or science; those who are likely to enter other technical areas (such as the health sciences) where they will make significant but limited use of math, engineering, or science; and those who will associate with science as citizens, not vocationally or professionally. The Foundation tries to give appropriate attention to all these students, but historically its support for future scientists, mathematicians, and engineers has been the most consistent.

APPENDIX C

U.S. Department of Education

Because the entire budget of the Department of Education is devoted to education activities, it is difficult to draw precise conclusions by contrasting Department of Education funds spent on education-related activities with Endowment funds spent for arts education.

It is useful to note, however, that the Department has directed a considerable portion of its resources to the support of education at the elementary and secondary levels, the same K-12 years that are the focus of the Arts Endowment's activities in arts education, and that the Department has provided high levels of support to improve teaching, increase literacy, and improve education in specific areas such as science and education. It also has provided significant support for the collection of data on the condition of education in the United States. These areas—the improvement of kindergarten through twelfth grade education, the strengthening of teaching, the enhancement of curricula in special subjects, and the support of research— are as important in arts education as they are in education as a whole.

In Fiscal Year 1987, the Department devoted 43 percent of its $19.3 billion budget to programs that support elementary and secondary education. The largest portion of this is the approximately $6.8 billion provided through programs which serve students with special needs. These children include the economically disadvantaged, children of limited English proficiency, Indian children, children who live in families that migrate, handicapped children, and neglected and delinquent children.

The Department allocates approximately $741 million of its budget to support several programs geared towards improving excellence in education. These include the Chapter 2 Block Grants to states, teacher training, improvement, and fellowship programs, literacy training, and funding to improve science and mathematics education.

The Department of Education recognizes the importance of arts education through a discretionary program within the Chapter 2 Block Grant for arts in education. In Fiscal Year 1987, $3.3 million was devoted to support two activities for Arts in Education Programs: (1) the Kennedy Center's education programs, which support a national network of state arts organizations and provide support for Kennedy Center Programs for Children and Youth and the American College Theatre Festival, both of which promote the expansion of opportunities for children and youth to participate in the arts; and (2) Very Special Arts, which develops programs that integrate the arts into the general education of disabled children and the lives of disabled adults.

In Fiscal Year 1987, $63.6 million was allocated to the Office of Educational Research and Improvement to collect data, conduct research, and disseminate information on the condition of education in the United States. While these funds are not exclusively used for elementary and secondary education, they play an important role because support for research and information is one of the principal ways the Department assists in improving educational performance.

Bibliography

Adler, M. 1982. *The Paideia Proposal.* New York, N.Y.: Macmillan.

Alliance for Arts Education, John F. Kennedy Center for the Performing Arts, and American Association of School Administrators. 1985. *Performing Together: The Arts and Education.* Washington, D.C.: American Association of School Administrators.

Alliance for Arts Education, John F. Kennedy Center for the Performing Arts. 1987. "State of the Arts: An Interchange Update," *Interchange* Summer Issue. Washington, D.C.: Alliance for Arts Education, John F. Kennedy Center for the Performing Arts.

American Association of Theatre for Youth, and American Association for Theatre in Secondary Education. 1987. *A Model Drama/Theatre Curriculum, Philosophy, Goals and Objectives.* New Orleans, La.: Anchorage Press.

Arkansas Board of Education. n.d. *Music, Arkansas Public School Course Content Guide.* Little Rock, Ar.: Arkansas Board of Education.

Arts, Education and Americans Panel, American Council for the Arts in Education. 1977. *Coming to Our Senses: The Significance of the Arts for American Education.* New York, N.Y.: McGraw Hill.

Association for Supervision and Curriculum Development, December 1987/January 1988. *Educational Leadership* 45. Alexandria, Va.: Association for Supervision and Curriculum Development.

Beethoven, J.; Davidson, J.; Nadon-Gabrion, C.; Ravosa, C.; Weikart, P.; and Bledsoe, D. 1988. *World of Music, Teacher Edition, Grade 5.* Morristown, N.J.: Silver, Burdett & Ginn Inc.

Bennett, W.J. September 1986. *First Lessons: A Report on Elementary Education.* Washington, D.C.: U.S. Government Printing Office.

———. 24 November 1986. "Remarks." Speech delivered at Conference of the National Association of Schools of Music, Colorado Springs, Co.

———. December 1987. *James Madison High School: A Curriculum for American Students.* Washington, D.C.: U.S. Department of Education.

Berman, P., and McLaughlin, M. W. 1978. *Federal Programs Supporting Educational Change: Volume VIII. Implementing and Sustaining Innovations.* Santa Monica, Ca.: The Rand Corporation.

Bloom, A. 1987. *The Closing of the American Mind.* New York, N.Y.: Simon and Schuster.

Boyer, E. 1983. *High School: A Report on Secondary Education in America.* New York, N.Y.: Harper and Row.

Bruner, J. 1986. *Actual Minds, Possible Worlds.* Cambridge, Ma. and London: Harvard University Press.

Carnegie Forum on Education and the Economy. 1986. *A Nation Prepared: Teachers for the 21st Century, The Report of the Task Force on Teaching as a Profession.* New York, N.Y.: Carnegie Corporation.

Center for Education Statistics, Office of Educational Research and Improvement. March 1987. "Teachers in Elementary and Secondary Education." CS87-324h. Washington, D.C.: U.S. Department of Education.

———. 1987. *Digest of Education Statistics.* Washington, D.C.: U.S. Government Printing Office.

———. February 1988. "Public School District Policies and Practices in Selected Aspects of Arts and Humanities Instruction." CS88.417. Washington, D.C.: U.S. Department of Education.

Chapman, L.H. 1982. *Instant Art Instant Culture: The Unspoken Policy for American Schools.* New York, N.Y. and London: Teachers College Press.

Chapman, L.H. 1985. *Teacher's Edition: Discover Art, Grade 4.* Worcester, Ma.: Davis Publications, Inc.

Cheney, L.V. 1987. *American Memory: A Report on the Humanities in the Nation's Public Schools.* Washington, D.C.: National Endowment for the Humanities.

Child Trends, Inc. May 1987. "Arts Education and the Public Schools. Overviews and Bibliographies of Documents Abstracted in the ERIC System on: Arts Education in General; Dance; Film; Literature; Music; Theatre; and Visual Arts." Prepared under contract C87-240 with the National Endowment for the Arts. Washington, D.C.: Child Trends, Inc.

Clarke, I.E. 1884. *Art and Industry, Instruction in Drawing Applied to Industrial and Fine Arts.* Washington, D.C.: U.S. Government Printing Office.

Coleman, J.S.; Campbell, E.Q.; Hobson, C.J.; McPartland, J.; Mood, A.M.; Weinfeld, F.D.; and York, R.L. 1966. *Equality of Educational Opportunity.* Washington, D.C.: U.S. Government Printing Office.

College Entrance Examination Board. 1983. *Academic Preparation for College, What Students Need to Know and Be Able to Do.* New York, N.Y.: College Entrance Examination Board.

_______ . 1985. *Academic Preparation in the Arts.* New York, N.Y.: College Entrance Examination Board.

Council of Chief State School Officers. August 1985. *Options and Opportunities in Arts Education.* Washington, D.C.: Council of Chief State School Officers.

_______ . September 1985. *Arts, Education and the States: A Survey of State Education Policies.* Washington, D.C.: Council of Chief State School Officers.

Crane, V. June 1981. *Research Report 84, Arts Education in Grades 6 Through 9: A National Survey of Arts Teachers and Supervisors.* Bloomington, In.: Research Communications, Inc. for the Arts Education Television Project Agency for Instructional Television.

Day, M.; Eisner, E.; Stake, R.; Wilson, B.; and Wilson, M. 1984. *Art History, Art Criticism, and Art Production: An Examination of Art Education in Selected School Districts, Volume II: Case Studies of Seven Selected Sites.* Santa Monica, Ca.: Prepared by the Rand Corporation for the Getty Center for Education in the Arts of the J. Paul Getty Trust.

Division of Curriculum Services, Office of Instructional Services. 1982. *Visual Arts Education Guidelines, K-12.* Atlanta, Ga.: Georgia Department of Education.

Dunkelman, M. 1985. *Grading the Advanced Placement Examination in History of Art* (No. 1800203.Y75P4.235502). Dayton, Oh.: Department of Art History, Wright State University.

Educational Research Service, Inc. 1983. *Effective Schools: A Summary of Research.* Arlington, Va.: Educational Research Service, Inc.

_______ . 1987. *Advanced Placement Course Description: Art.* New York, N.Y.: College Entrance Examination Board.

_______ . 1987. *Advanced Placement Course Description: Music.* New York, N.Y.: College Entrance Examination Board.

Efland, A. 1977. *Planning Art Education in the Middle/Secondary Schools of Ohio.* Columbus, Oh.: State of Ohio Department of Education.

Eisner, E.W. 1985. *The Educational Imagination* 2nd ed. New York, N.Y.: Macmillan Company.

Erbes, R.L. 1986. *Certification Practices and Trends in Music Teacher Education 1985-86.* Reston, Va.: Music Educators National Conference.

Evaluation Technologies, Inc. 1984. "Course Offerings in the Arts and the Humanities at the Secondary School Level." Prepared under Contract 300-83-0037, U.S. Department of Education. Washington, D.C.

Fiske, E.B. 1987. "The Push for Smarter Textbooks." *New York Times Magazine* Education Supplement, 18 May 1987.

Getty Center for Education in the Arts. 1985. *Beyond Creating: The Place for Art in America's Schools.* Los Angeles, Ca.: Getty Center for Education in the Arts.

Goodlad, J.I. 1984. *A Place Called School, Prospects for the Future.* New York, N.Y.: McGraw-Hill Book Company.

Goodman, N. 1984. *Of Mind and Other Matters.* Cambridge, Ma.: Harvard University Press.

Goodman, N. 1978. *Ways of Worldmaking.* Indianapolis, In. and Cambridge, Ma.: Hackett Publishing Company.

Government of Japan. 1983. *Course of Study for Elementary Schools in Japan* Notification No. 155 of Ministry of Education, Science and Culture. Japan: Educational and Cultural Exchange Division, UNESCO and International Affairs Department, Science and International Affairs Bureau, Ministry of Education, Science and Culture.

Hirsch, E.D., Jr. 1987. *Cultural Literacy, What Every American Needs to Know.* Boston, Ma.: Houghton Mifflin Company.

Hoffa, H. 1970. *An Analysis of Recent Research Conferences in Art Education* Final Report, Project No. 8e093, Grant No. OEG5-9-245093-022. Washington, D.C.: Bureau of Research, Office of Education, U.S. Department of Health, Education, and Welfare.

Holmes Group. 1986. *Tomorrow's Teachers: A Report of the Holmes Group.* East Lansing, Mi.: The Holmes Group, Inc.

Hypes, J., ed. 1978. *Discover Dance: Teaching Modern Dance in Secondary Schools.* Washington, D.C.: National Dance Association, an Association of the American Alliance for Health, Physical Education and Recreation.

Illinois State Board of Education, Department of School Improvement Services. 1986. *State Goals for Learning and Sample Learning Objectives, Fine Arts, Grades 3,6,8,10,12.* Springfield, Il.: Illinois State Board of Education.

Janson, H.W. 1986. *History of Art* 3rd ed. N.Y.: Henry N. Abrams, Inc.

Johnson, R. and Bone, J. 1986. *Understanding the Film, an Introduction to Film Appreciation.* Lincolnwood, Il.: National Textbook Company.

Lehman, P. R. 1985. *The Class of 2001, Coping with the Computer Bandwagon.* Reston, Va.: Music Educators National Conference.

Lehman, P. R. 1987. *Music in Today's Schools: Rationale and Commentary.* Reston, Va.: The Music Educators National Conference.

Mahlmann, J.J.; Hope, S.; and Krakora, J. eds. September/October 1986. *Design for Arts in Education* Vol. 88, No. 1. Washington, D.C.: Heldref Publications.

Marsh, M.V.; Rinehart, C.; and Savage, E. 1983. *MacMillan Music: The Spectrum of Music with Related Arts* Teacher's Annotated Edition, Level 5. New York, N.Y.: Macmillan.

Medoff, M. April 1987. "Swan Song." *Dramatics.* Cincinnati, Oh.: International Thespian Society.

Meske, E.B.; Pautz, M.P.; Andress, B.; and Willman, F. 1988. *Holt-Music* Teacher's Edition, Grade 5. New York, N.Y.: Holt, Rinehart and Winston.

Mills, E.A., and Thomson, D.R. 1986. *A National Survey of Art(s) Education, 1984-85: A National Report on the State of the Arts in the States.* Reston, Va.: National Art Education Association.

Murphy, J., and Jones, L. 1976. *Research in Arts Education, A Federal Chapter* Publication No. OE 76-02000. Washington, D.C.: U.S. Department of Health, Education, and Welfare.

Music Educators National Conference. 1984. *Music and Music Education: Data and Information.* Reston, Va.: Music Educators National Conference.

_______ . 1985. *Arts in Schools State by State.* Reston, Va.: Music Educators National Conference.

_______ . 1986. *The School Music Program: Description and Standards* Second Edition. Reston, Va.: Music Educators National Conference.

Music Educators National Conference, et. al. 1986. *K-12 Arts Education in the United States: Present Context, Future Needs.* Reston, Va.: Music Educators National Conference.

_______ . November 1986. *The New National Endowment for the Arts Arts-in-Education Program.* Reston, Va.: Music Educators National Conference.

National Art Education Association. n.d. *Quality Art Education: A Checklist Developed for Elementary Principals.* Reston, Va.: National Art Education Association.

National Assembly of Local Arts Agencies. 1987. "1987 NALAA Member Survey." Washington, D.C.: N.A.L.A.A.

National Assembly of State Arts Agencies, Katz, J. ed. 1988. *Arts and Education Handbook: A Guide to Productive Collaborations.* Washington, D.C.: N.A.S.A.A.

National Assessment of Educational Progress. February 1974. *The First National Assessment of Musical Performance* Report 03-MU-01. Denver, Co.: Education Commission of the States.

_______ . August 1974. *The First Music Assessment: An Overview* Report 03-MU-00. Washington, D.C.: Superintendent of Documents, U.S. Government Printing Office.

_______ . September 1974. *An Assessment of Attitudes Toward Music* Report 03-MU-03. Washington, D.C.: Superintendent of Documents, U.S. Government Printing Office.

_______ . November 1981. *Music 1971-79: Results From the Second National Music Assessment* Report 10-MU-01. Denver, Co.: Education Commission of the States.

_______ . December 1981. *Results From The Second National Art Assessment.* Report 10-A-01. Denver, Co.: Education Commission of the States.

_______ . 1985. *The Reading Report Card.* Princeton, N.J.: Educational Testing Service.

_______ . 1986. *The Writing Report Card.* Princeton, N.J.: Educational Testing Service.

National Association of Schools of Art and Design. 1987. *National Association of Schools of Art and Design Handbook 1987-1988.* Reston, Va.: National Association of Schools of Art and Design.

National Association of Schools of Music. 1987. *National Association of Schools of Music, 1987-1988 Handbook.* Reston, Va.: N.A.S.M.

_______ . 1987. *Proceedings, 62nd Annual Meeting* No. 75. Reston, Va.: N.A.S.M.

National Association of Schools of Theatre. 1986. *Handbook 1987-1989.* Reston, Va.: N.A.S.T.

National Association of Secondary School Principals. 1984. *The Mood of American Youth.* Reston, Va.: National Association of Secondary School Principals.

National Commission on Excellence in Education. April 1983. *A Nation at Risk: The Imperative for Educational Reform.* Washington, D.C.: U.S. Government Printing Office.

National Congress of Parents and Teachers. 1985. *Children and the Arts: What Your PTA Can Do.* Chicago, Il.: N.C.P.T.

_______ . 1985. *The Best in Children's Art.* Chicago, Il.: N.C.P.T.

National Governors' Association. 1986. *Time for Results, the Governors' 1991 Report on Education.* Washington, D.C.: National Governors' Association.

North Carolina State Board of Education. January 1986. *The Basic Education Program for North Carolina's Public Schools.* Raleigh, N.C.: North Carolina State Board of Education.

Office of Educational Research and Improvement. *Japanese Education Today, A Report from the U.S. Study of Education in Japan.* Washington, D.C.: U.S. Department of Education.

Oklahoma State Department of Education. June 1985. *Curriculum Review Handbook: The Arts, Includes Student Outcomes for: Art, Music, Dance, Drama/Theatre, and Comprehensive Arts.* Oklahoma City, Ok.: Oklahoma State Department of Education.

Orend, R.J. April 1987. "Socialization in the Arts." Prepared under Contract No. C86-179 for the National Endowment for the Arts, Washington, D.C.

Pappalardo, M. 1987. "A Long-Range Study of Dance Programs in the Public School Systems of the United States, Grades 7 Through 12: A Draft Report." Prepared for the National Dance Association, Reston, Va.

Piaget, J. 1972. "Some Aspects of Operations." *Play and Development,* edited by M.W. Piers. New York, N.Y.: Norton.

Robinson, J.P.; Keegan, C.A.; Hanford, T.; Triplett, T.A., University of Maryland, SRC. 1985. "Public Participation in the Arts: Final Report on the 1982 Survey." Prepared in fulfillment of Grant 2-4050-003, Research Division, National Endowment for the Arts, Washington, D.C.

Robinson, J.P.; Keegan, C.A.; Karth, M.; Triplett, T.A. University of Maryland, SRC. 1987. "Survey of Public Participation in the Arts: 1985 Vol. 1, Project Report." Prepared under Cooperative Agreement NEA CA 85-24 with the National Endowment for the Arts, Washington, D.C.

Salisbury, B.T. 1986. *Theatre Arts in the Elementary Classroom, Grade Four through Grade Six.* New Orleans, La.: Anchorage Press, Inc.

Salome, R.A. and Marantz, K.A., eds. 1985 and 1986. *Studies in Art Education: A Journal of Issues and Research in Art Education* 27, No. 3, 2 & 1. Reston, Va.: The National Art Education Association.

Sizer, T.R. 1984. *Horace's Compromise: The Dilemma of the American High School.* Boston: Houghton Mifflin.

Smith, R.A. 1986. *Excellence in Art Education: Ideas and Initiatives.* Reston, Va. National Art Education Association.

Spillane, R.R. September 1987. "Arts Education Is Not a Frill!" *Updating School Board Policies* 18, National School Boards Association.

Study Group, U.S. Department of Education, and National Academy of Education. 1987. *The Nation's Report Card: Improving the Assessment of Student Achievement.* Cambridge, Ma.: National Academy of Education.

Taylor, J., ed. 1985. *Journal of Research in Music Education, Winter 1984* 32, No. 4. Reston, Va.: Music Educators National Conference.

Taylor, J. ed. *Journal of Research in Music Education, Table of Contents.* (1987, Vol. 35, No. 1 & 2; 1986, Vol. 34, No. 1-3; 1985, Vol 33, No 1-4; 1984, Vol. 32, No. 1-4; 1983, Vol 31, No. 1-4). Reston, Va.: Music Educators National Conference.

Working Group on the Arts in Higher Education. 1987. *Teacher Education in the Arts Disciplines, A Statement of the Working Group on the Arts in Higher Education.* Reston, Va.: Working Group on the Arts in Higher Education.

Credits for Unidentified Interior Photos

Pages x, 28, 46, 88, 92, 132, 170: Montgomery County (Maryland) Public Schools. William Mills, photographer.
Page 149: Children wait for doors to open for a Chicago Symphony concert. Robert Savely, photographer.
Page 64: An actor signs his dialogue at the Crosswalk Theatre. Walter S. Silver, photographer.
Page 68: Warner Avenue School, Los Angeles Unified School District, Los Angeles, California.
Page 104: Niles Township High Schools, North Division, Skokie, Illinois.

Individuals Who Contributed Background Information for the Report

Denise Anderson/Chris Appleford/Robert August/Marsha Besch/Gretchen Boyer/David Boyle/Pat Brown/Richard Bundy/Kimberly N. Camp/Ann Caulkins/Sarah Chapman/Jackie Cocke/Julie Cook/Rolaine Copland/Yolanda Cruz/Bill Dawson/Michael Day/Richard Dornek/Boyd Dressler/Jo Driebelis/Alexandra Fogel/Barbara Frank/Ruth Gassett/Joe W. Giles/Dennis Grabowski/Preston Hancock/Margie R. Hanson/Thomas A. Hatfield/Peter Hermans/Linda Hill/Mary Honetschlager/Sam Hope/Pat House/Dianne S. Howe/David Humphrey/Christine Huss/Norbert W. Irvine/Andrea Karpati/Eldon Katter/Jonathan Katz/Harold G. Keaton/Myrtle Kerr/Linda Kokinis/Archie LaPointe/Richard W. Layman/Franklin Lewis/Pat Lomock/Robert Lynch/Laura Magee/John Mahlmann/Vivian Makhmaltchi/Roger McGaughey/John McLaughlin/William Mills/Jeanne Moore/David Morgan/Ina Mullis/Catherine Nadon-Gabrion/Mitsuie Nagamachi/Sheila G. Newman/Marlene Pennington/Ruth Perlin/Richard Pioli/W. J. Raijmakers/Martin Rayala/Becky Duval Reese/Joe Reis/Tom Ritenbaugh/Jeanne Rollins/James W. Rooker/Stef Runyan/Joanne Rutkowski/Cheryl Sackman/Mark Schubart/Julie Smith/Ralph A. Smith/John D. Sommer/Rosann Stanko/Jerry Stashak/Dan Steinel/Scott Stoner/Linda L. Stowers/Tomiji Sugawa/Edmund Sullivan/Alice Swanson/Dennis Swanson/Martha Thurmen/Jerry Tollifson/Marcil Tressler/Alice Trimmer/James L. Tucker, Jr./Marjo Van Hoorn/Roberta Volkmann/Karen Weeks/Kim Wheetley/Marjorie Wilson/Joyce E. Wright/Nicholas Zill/Enid Zimmerman

This is not an exhaustive list. The contributions of others not noted here, which helped to make this report possible, are greatly appreciated.

Design by Maria Josephy Schoolman, Capital Ideas